ADHD COLOURING BOOK

A Stress Free
Hyper-Focusing Activity
For Any and All
Overwhelmed Beings

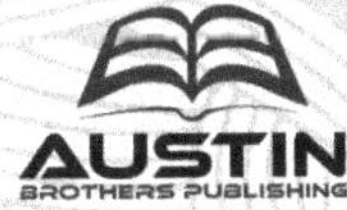

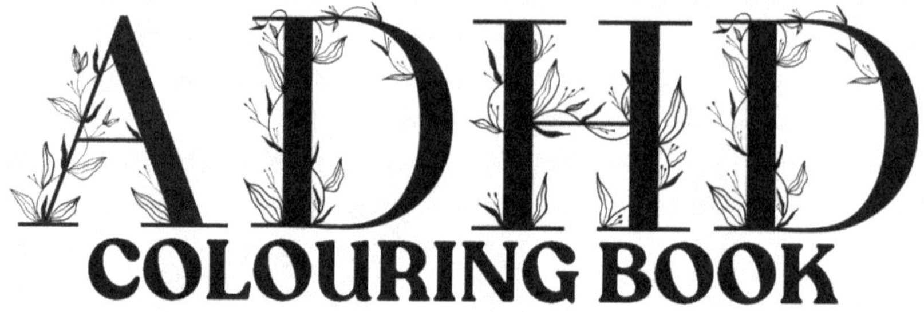

COLOURING BOOK

Published in the United States
by Austin Brothers Publishing

www.abpbooks.com

Printed in the United States of America
2025 -- First Edition

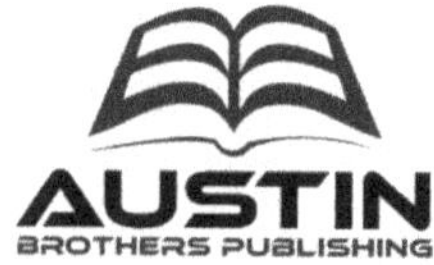

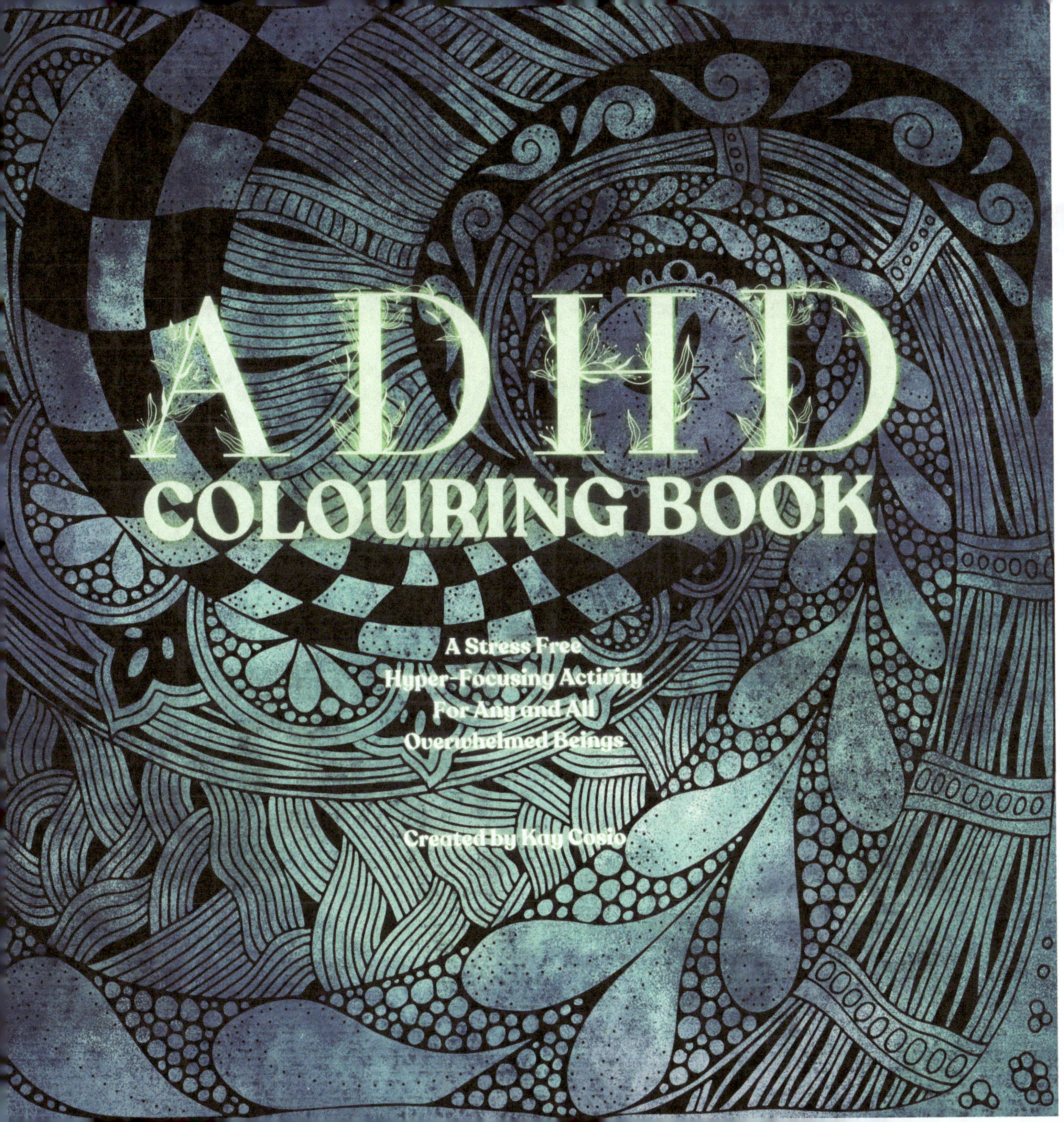
ADHD
COLOURING BOOK
A Stress Free
Hyper-Focusing Activity
For Any and All
Overwhelmed Beings
Created by Kay Cosio

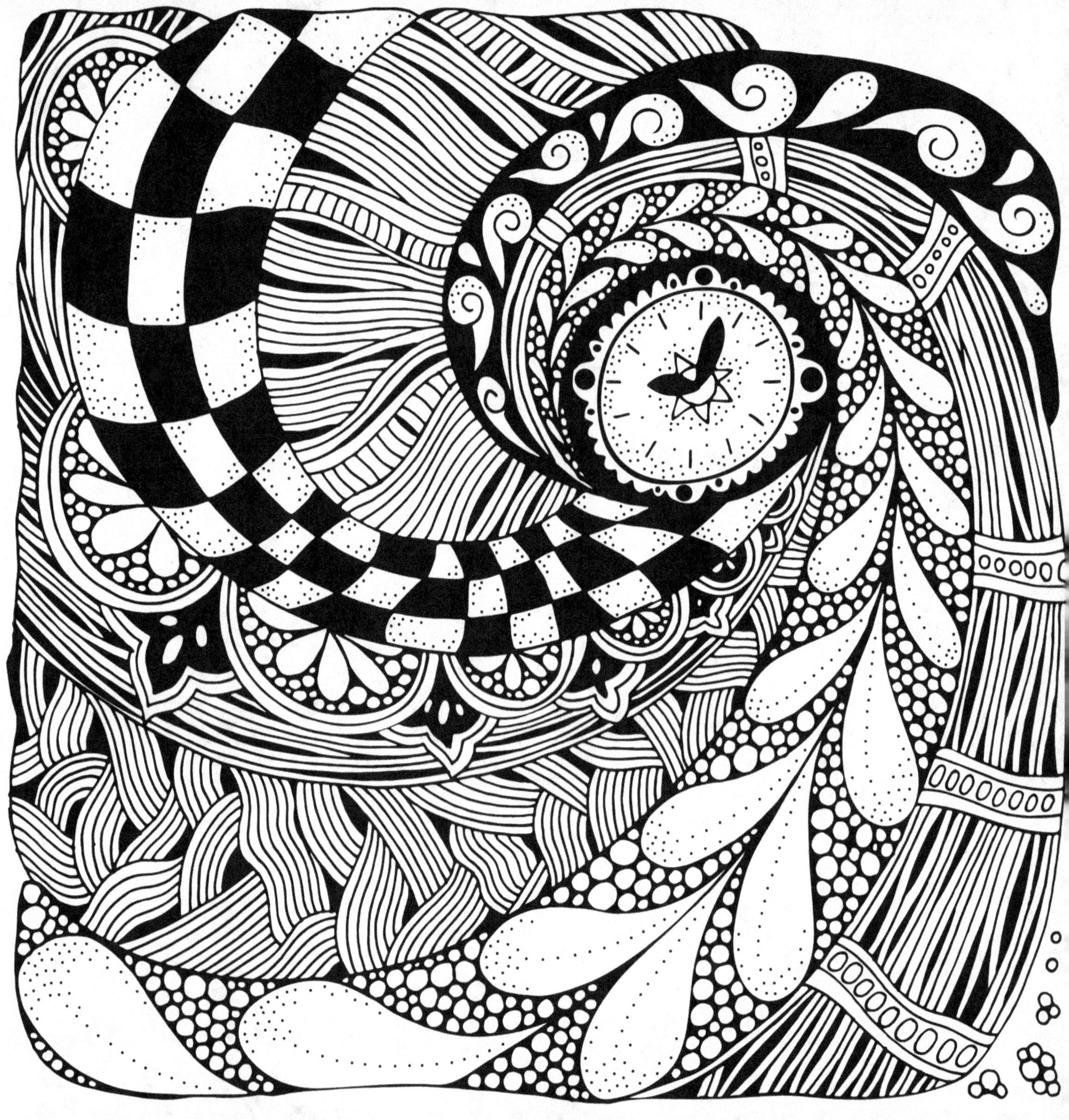

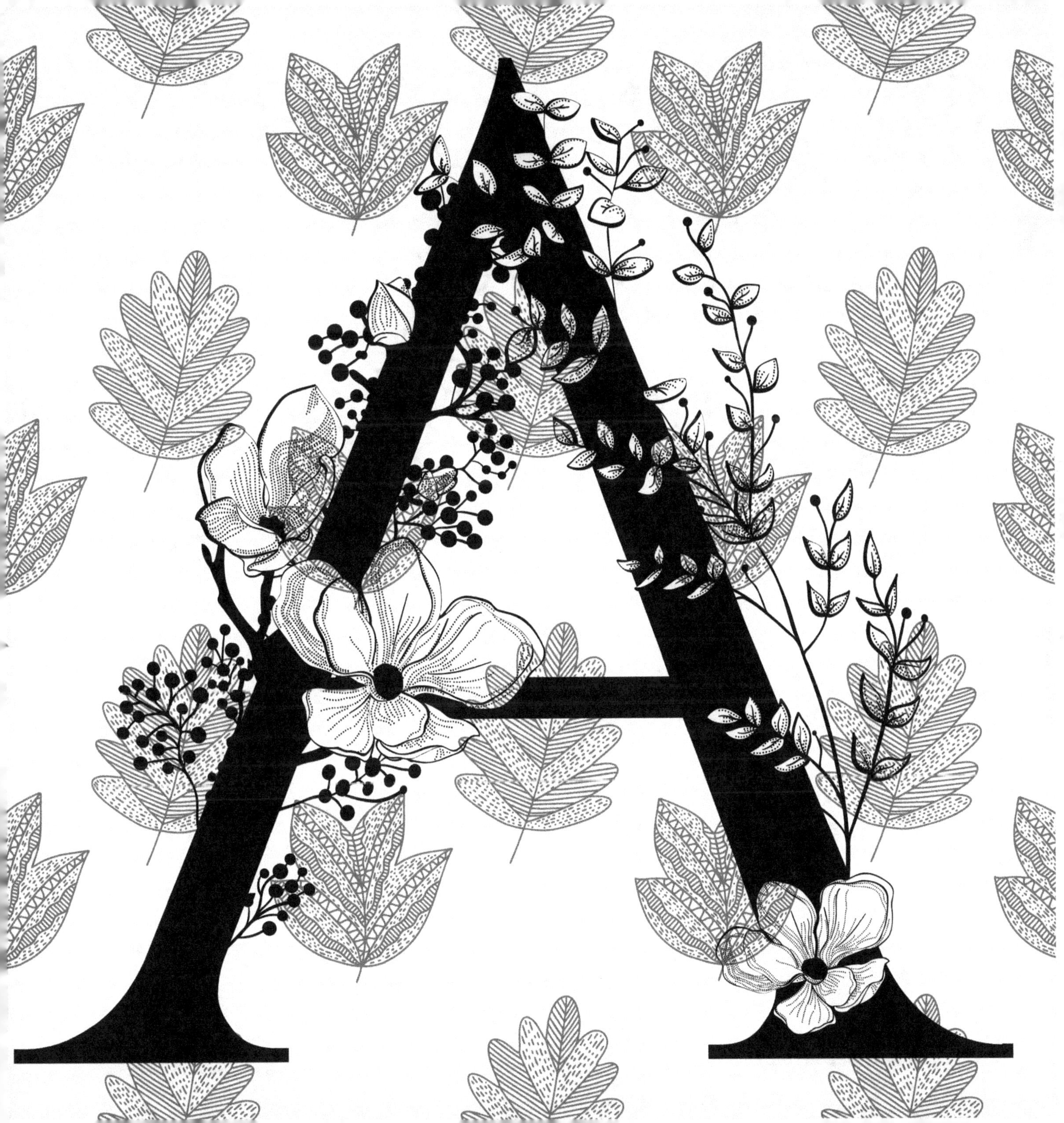

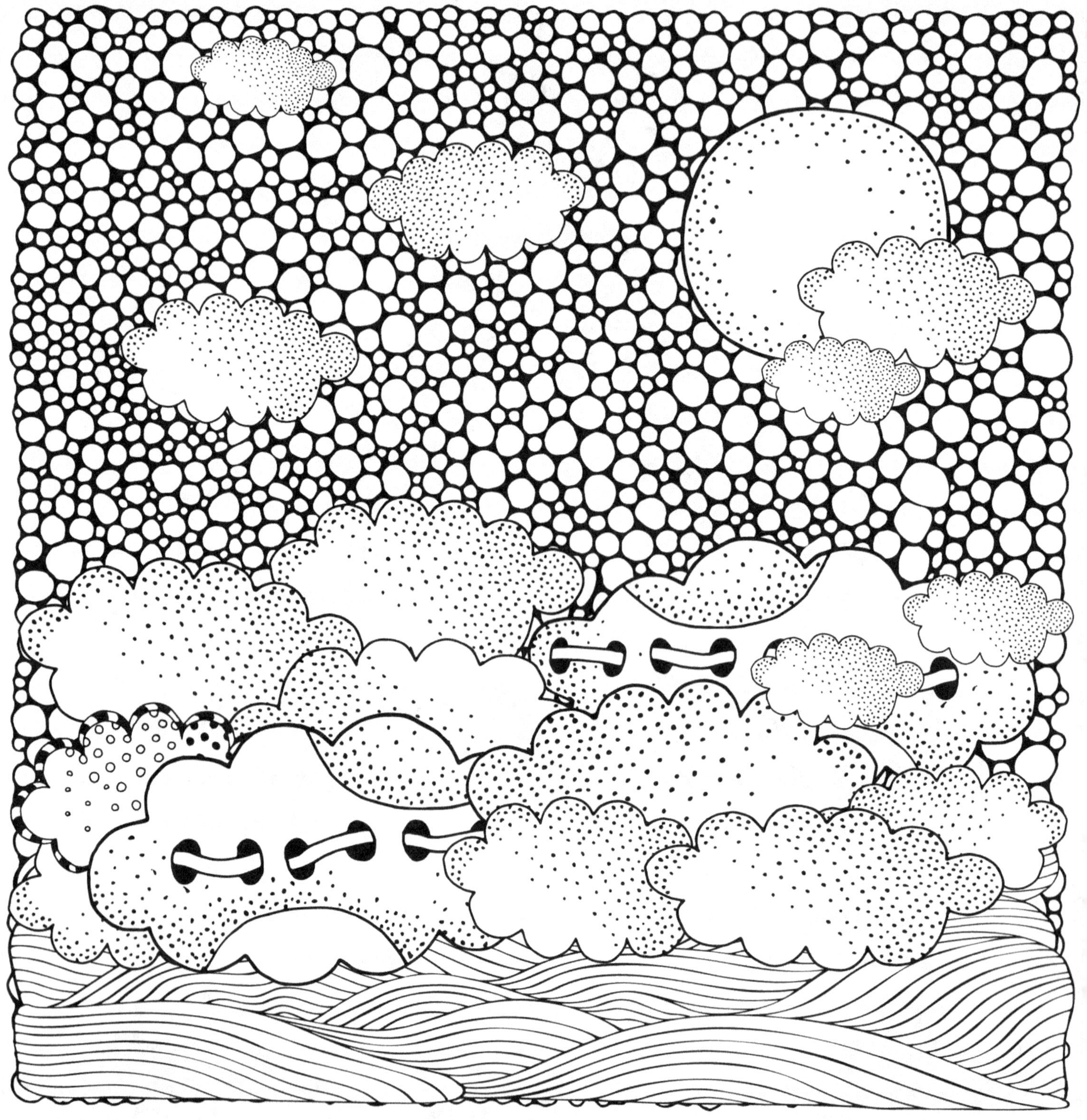

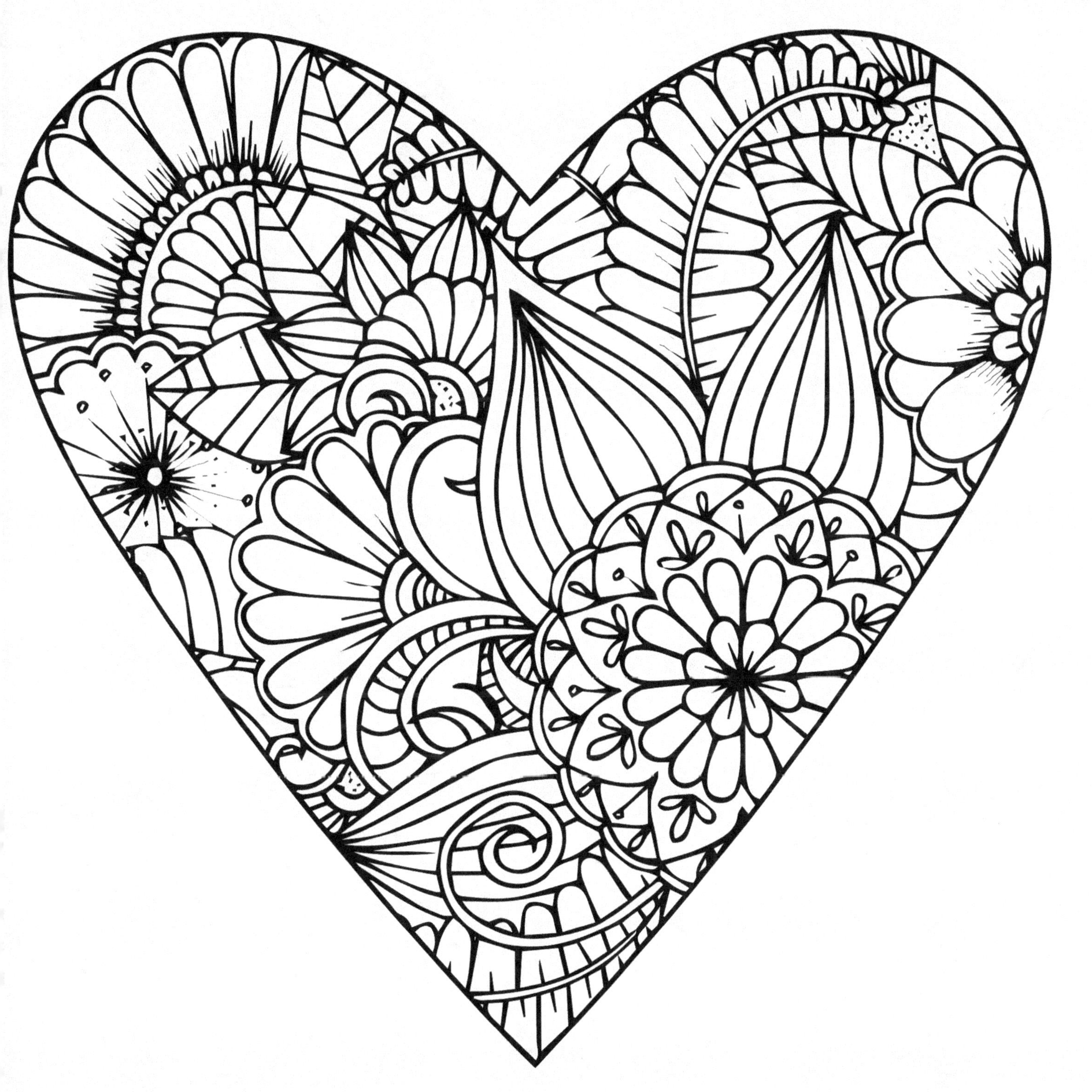

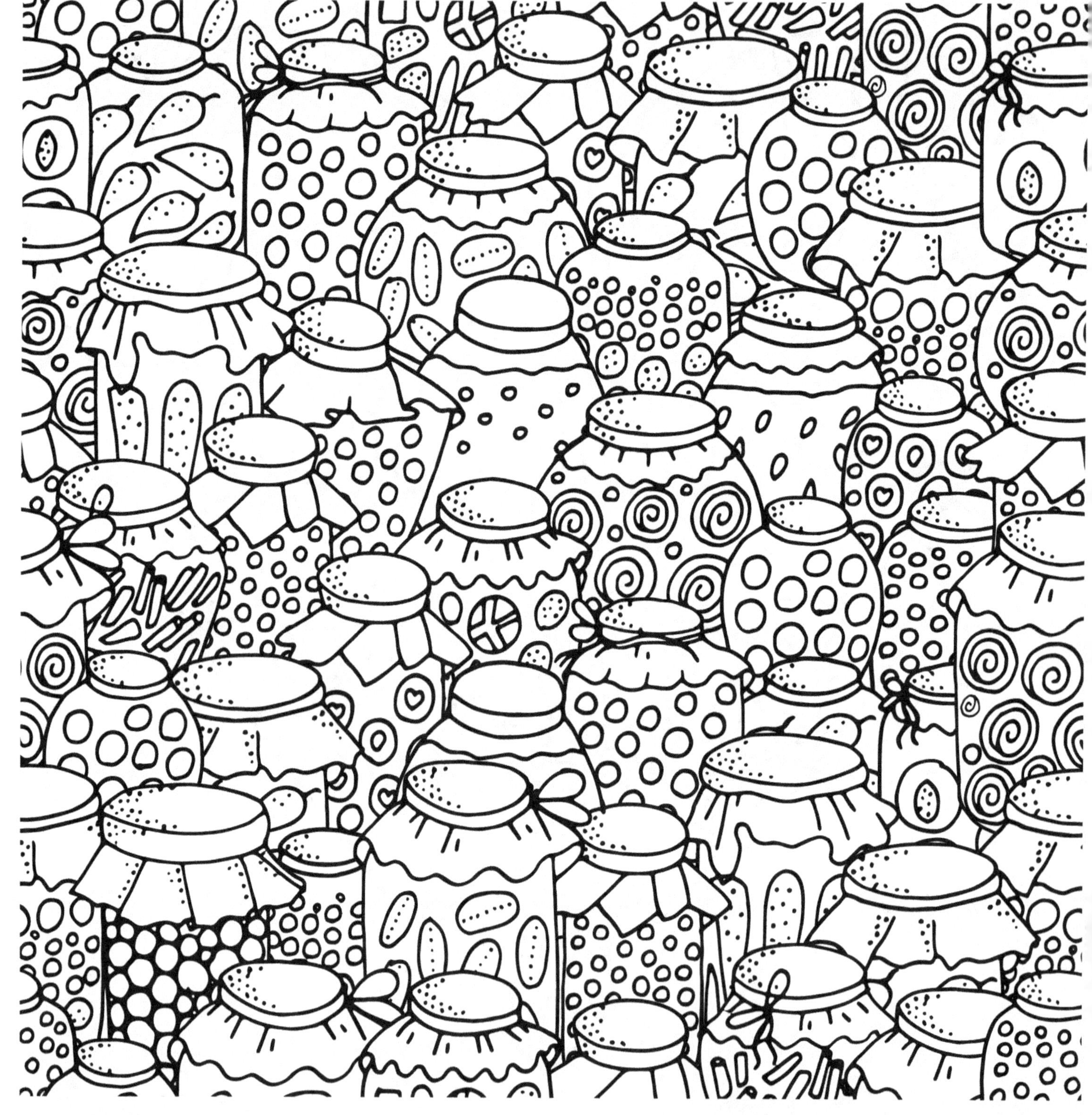

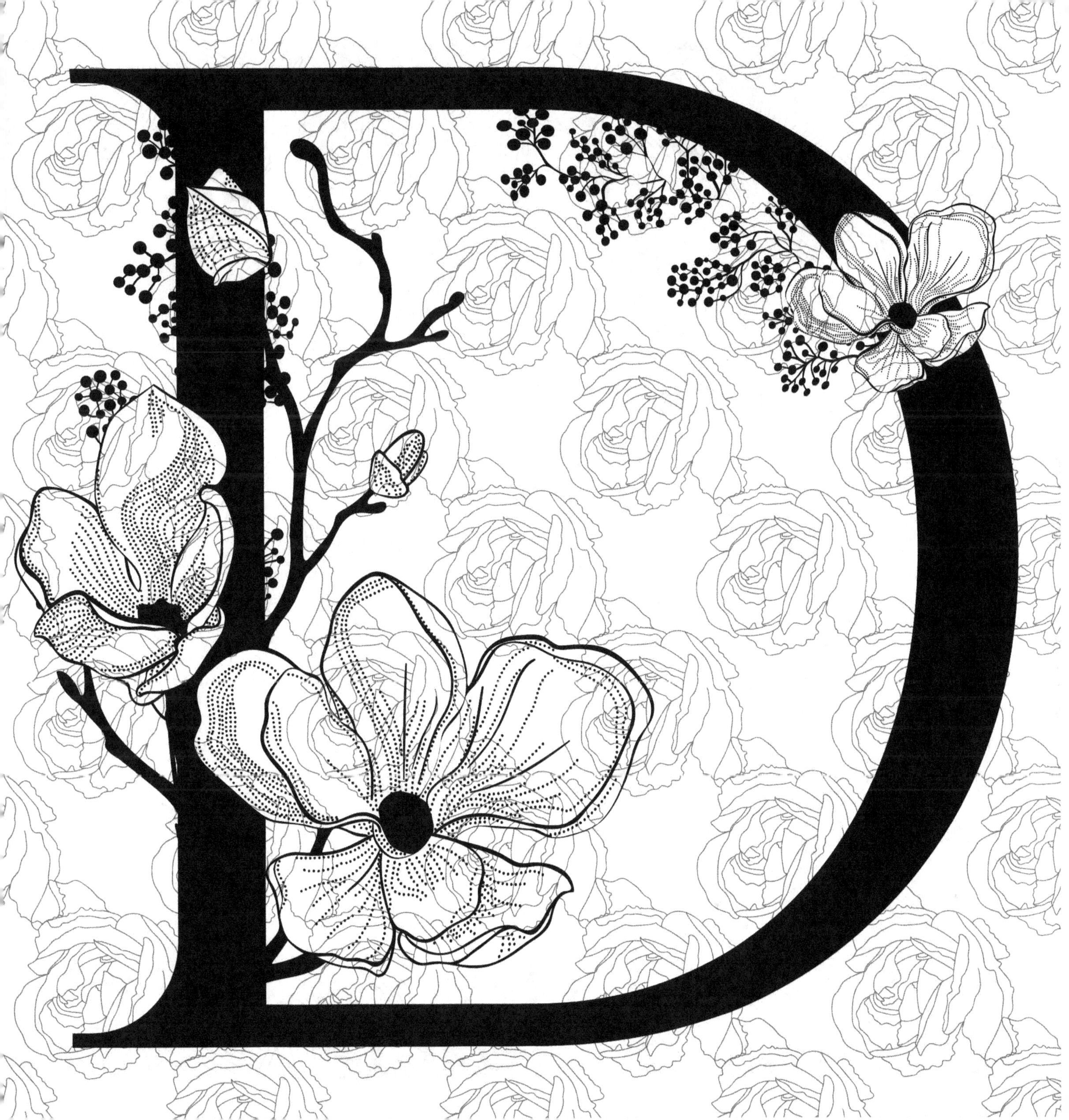

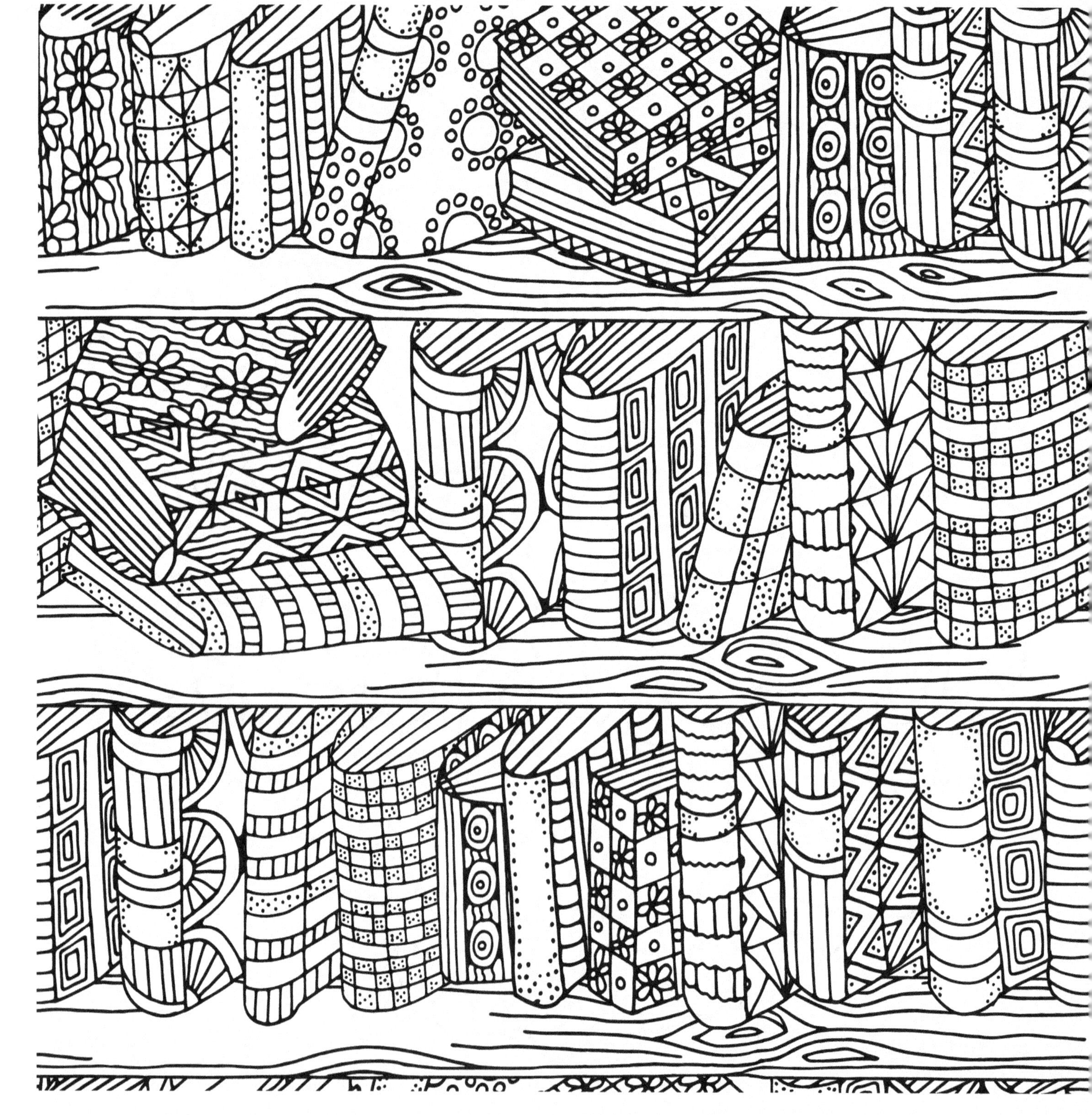

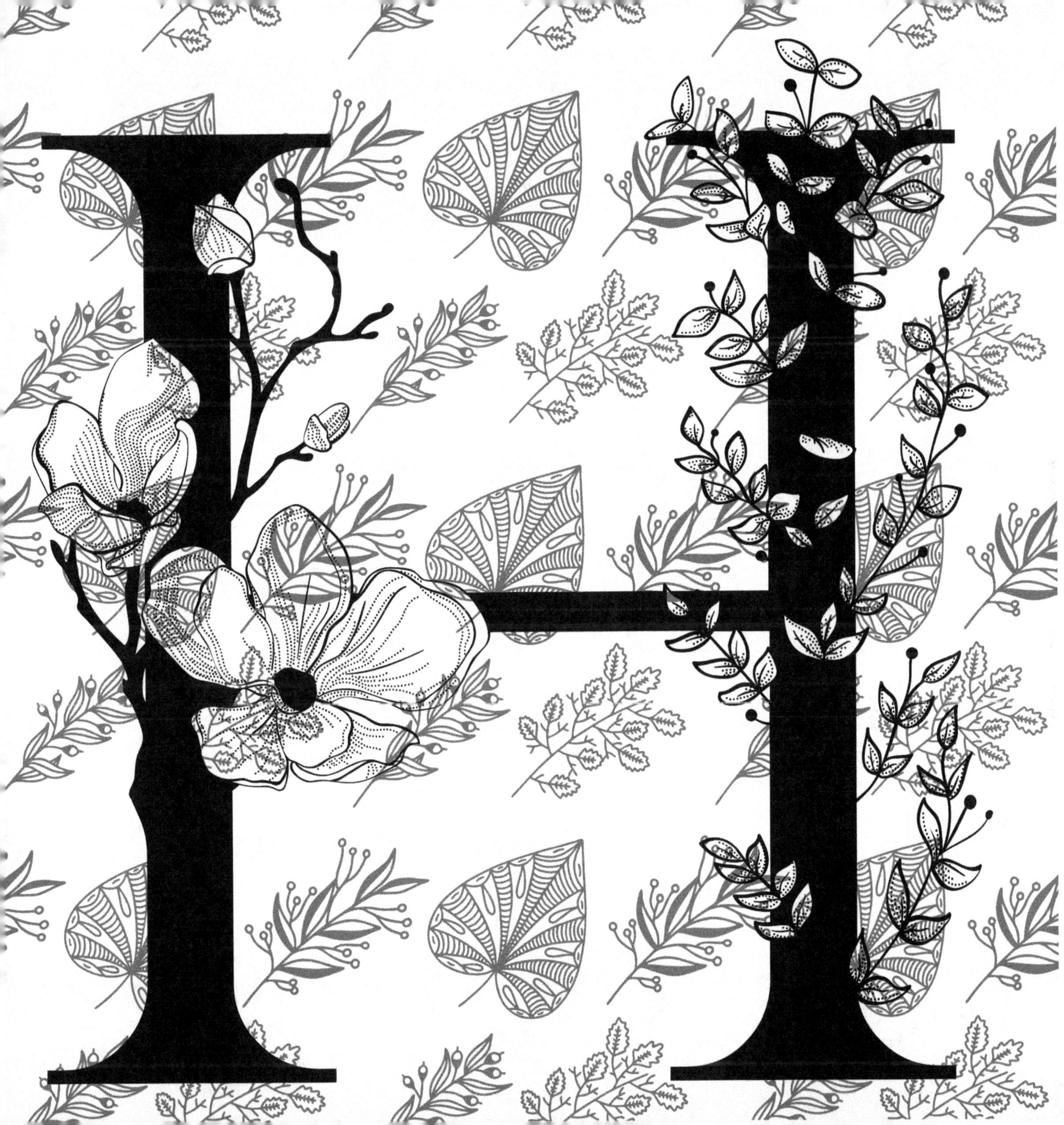

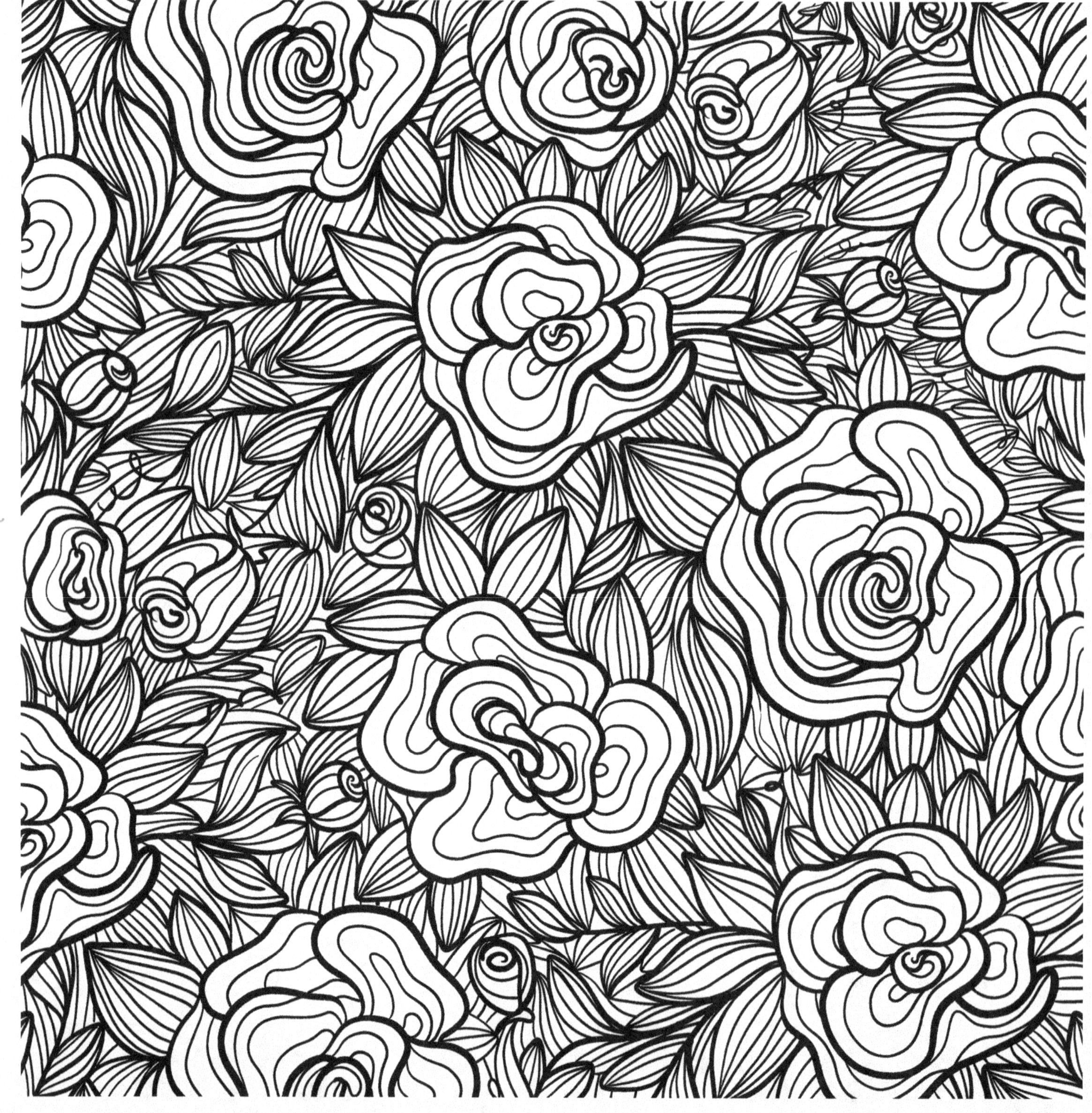

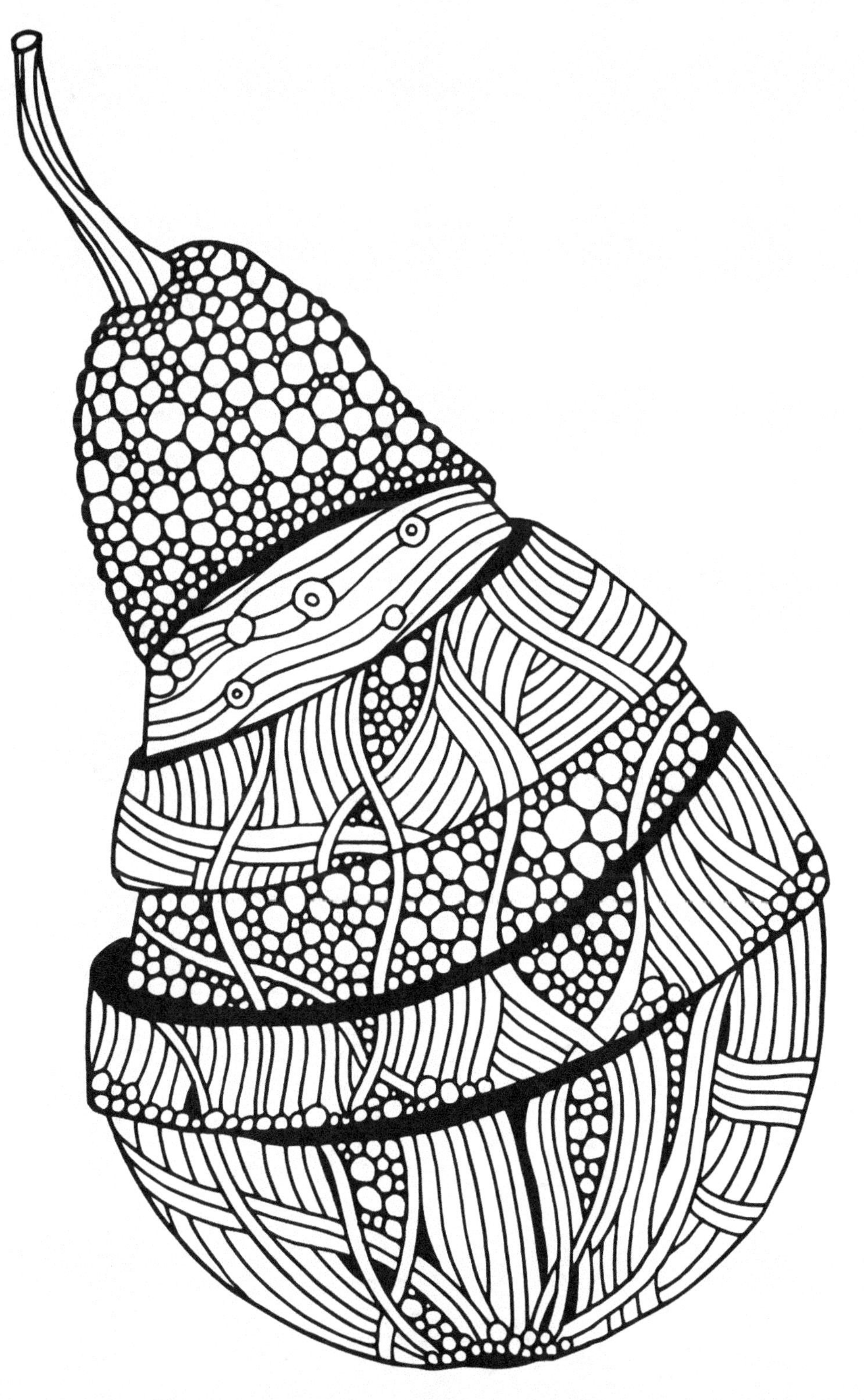

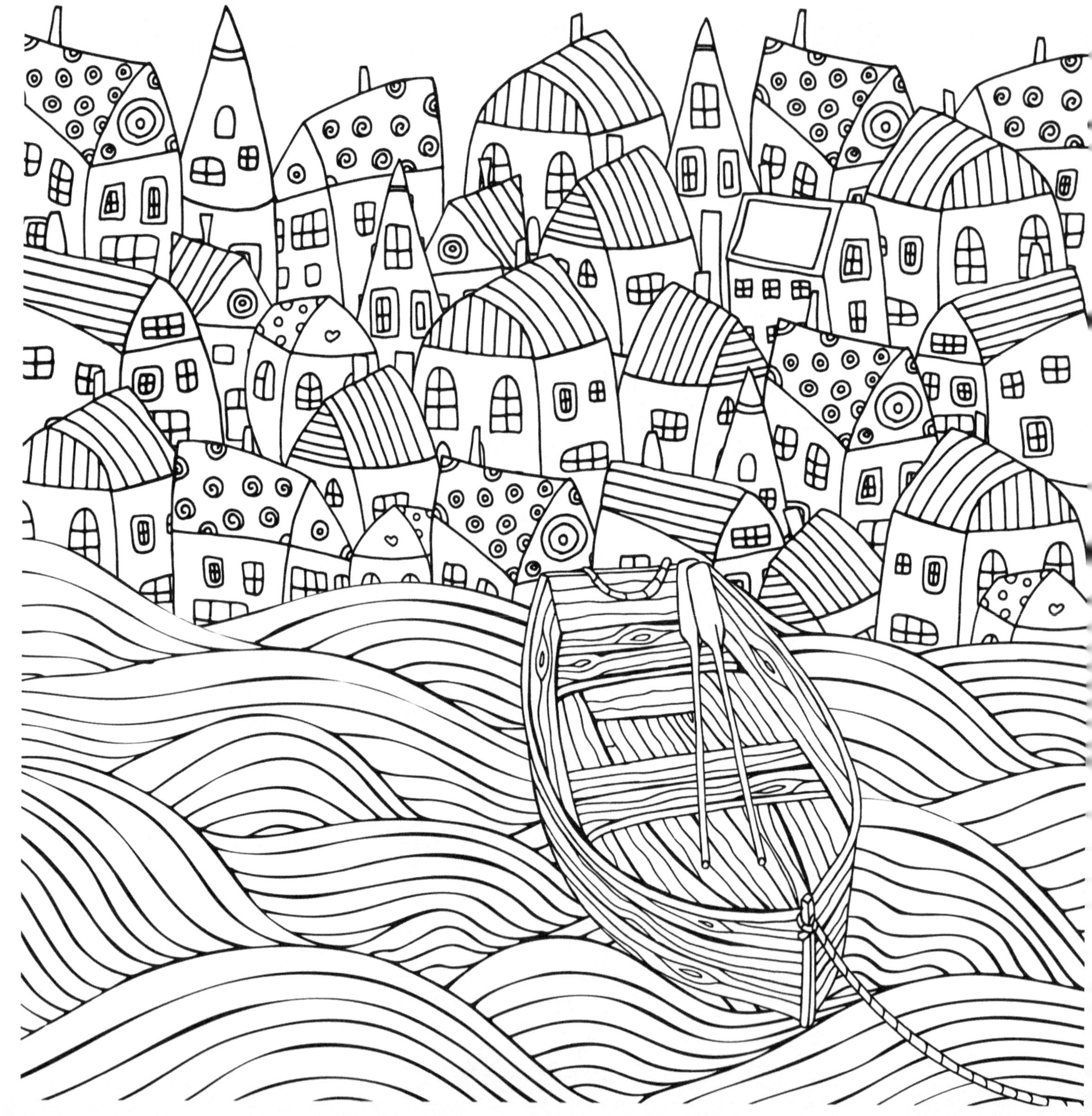

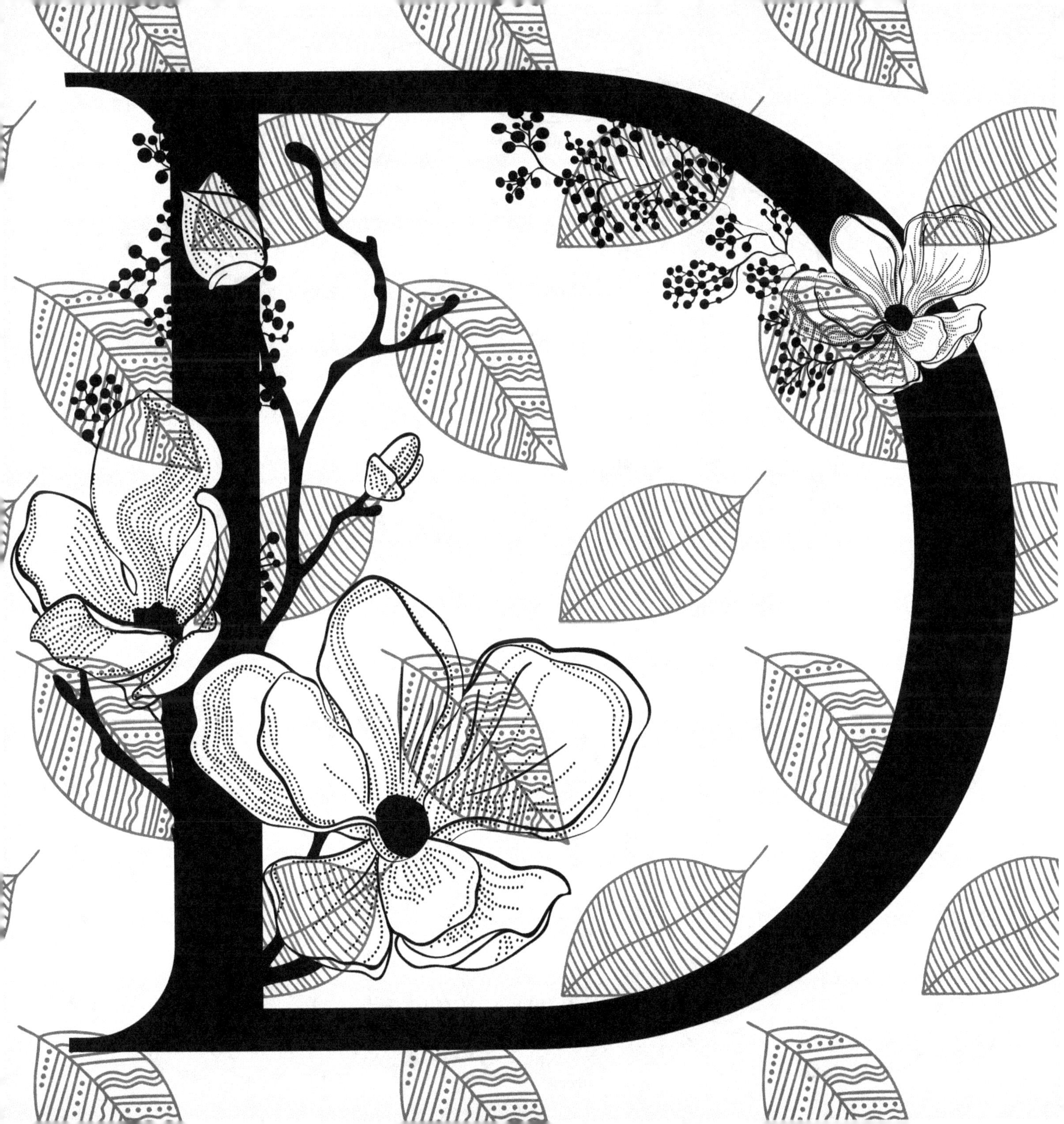

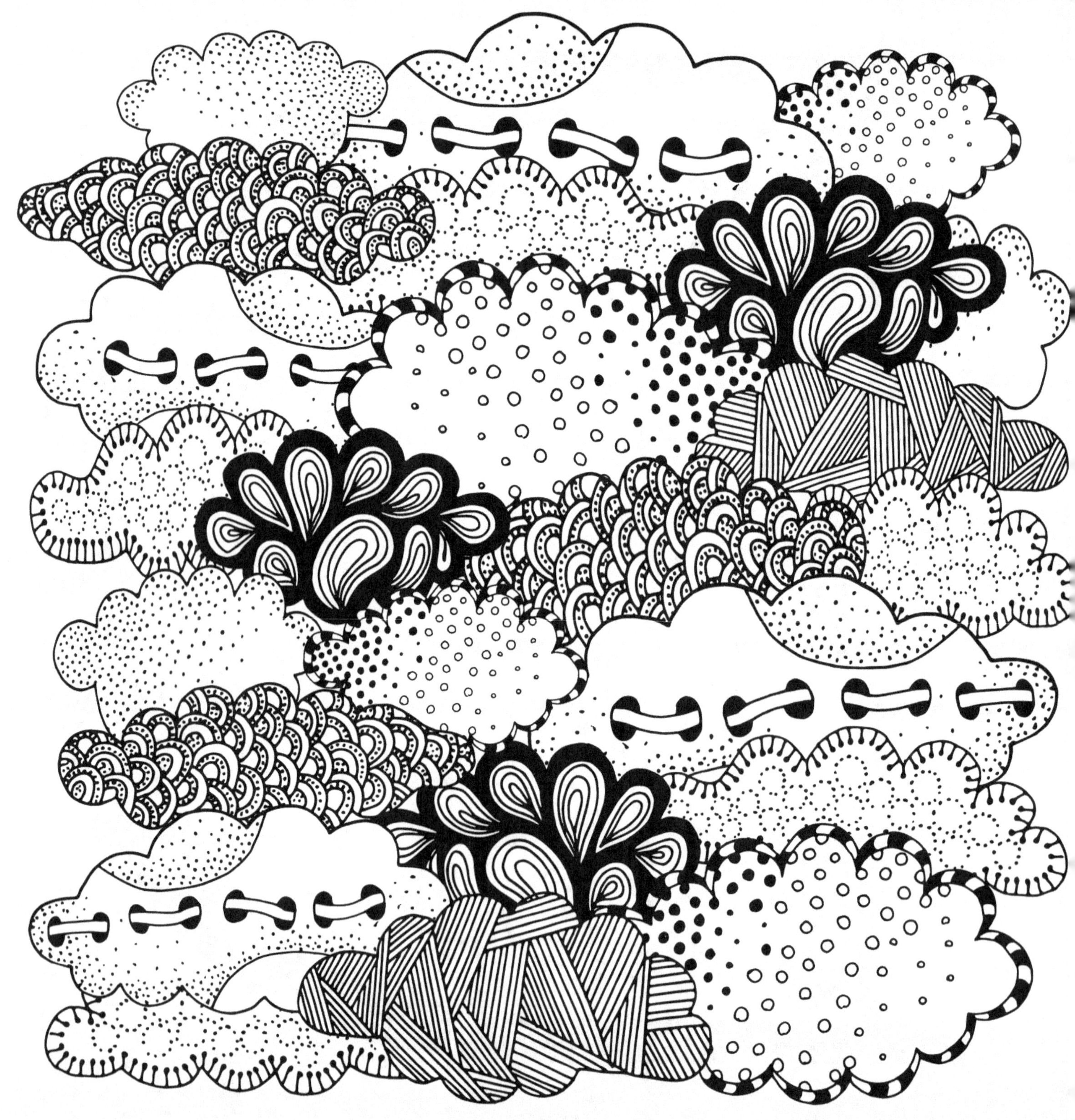

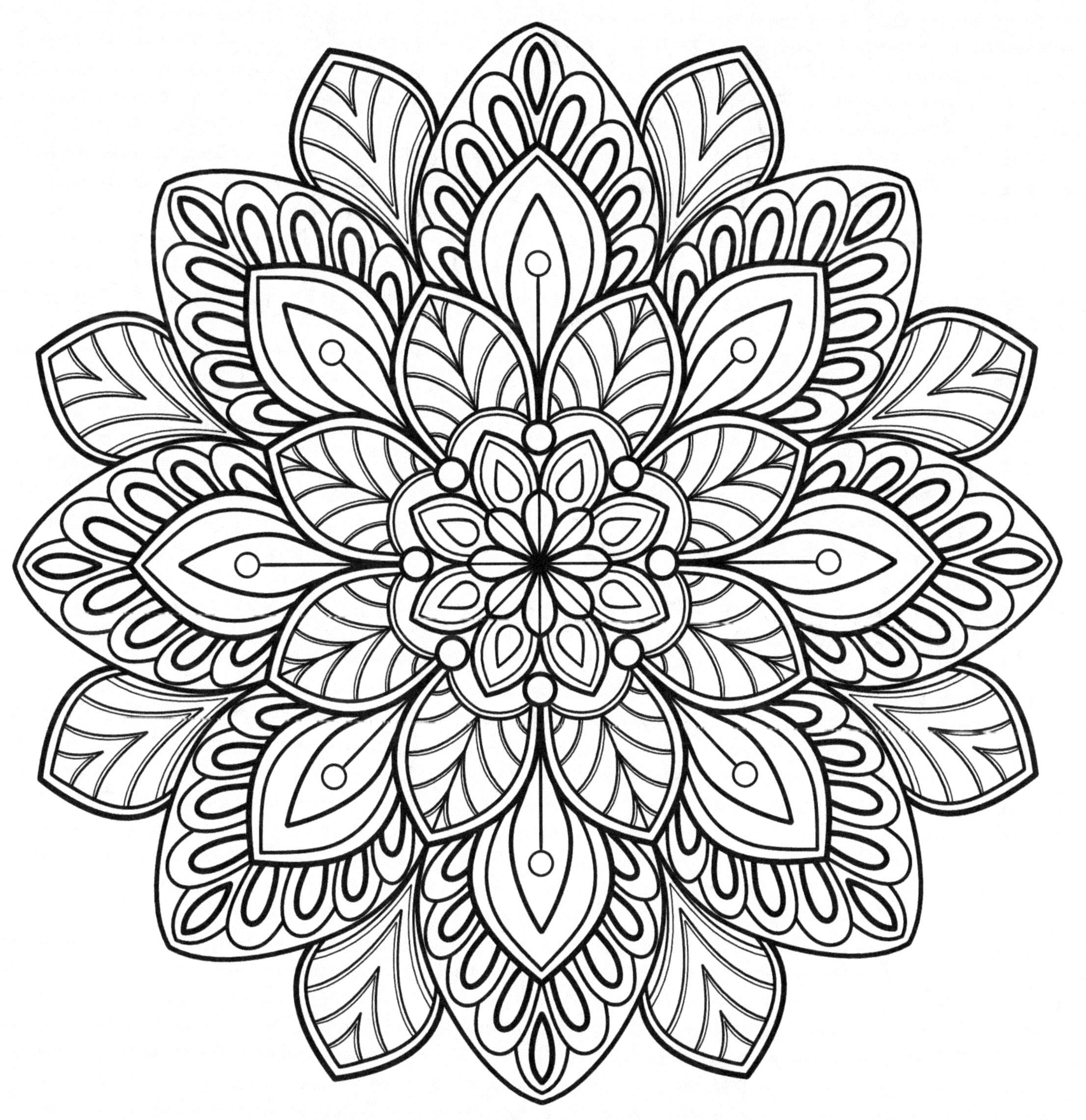

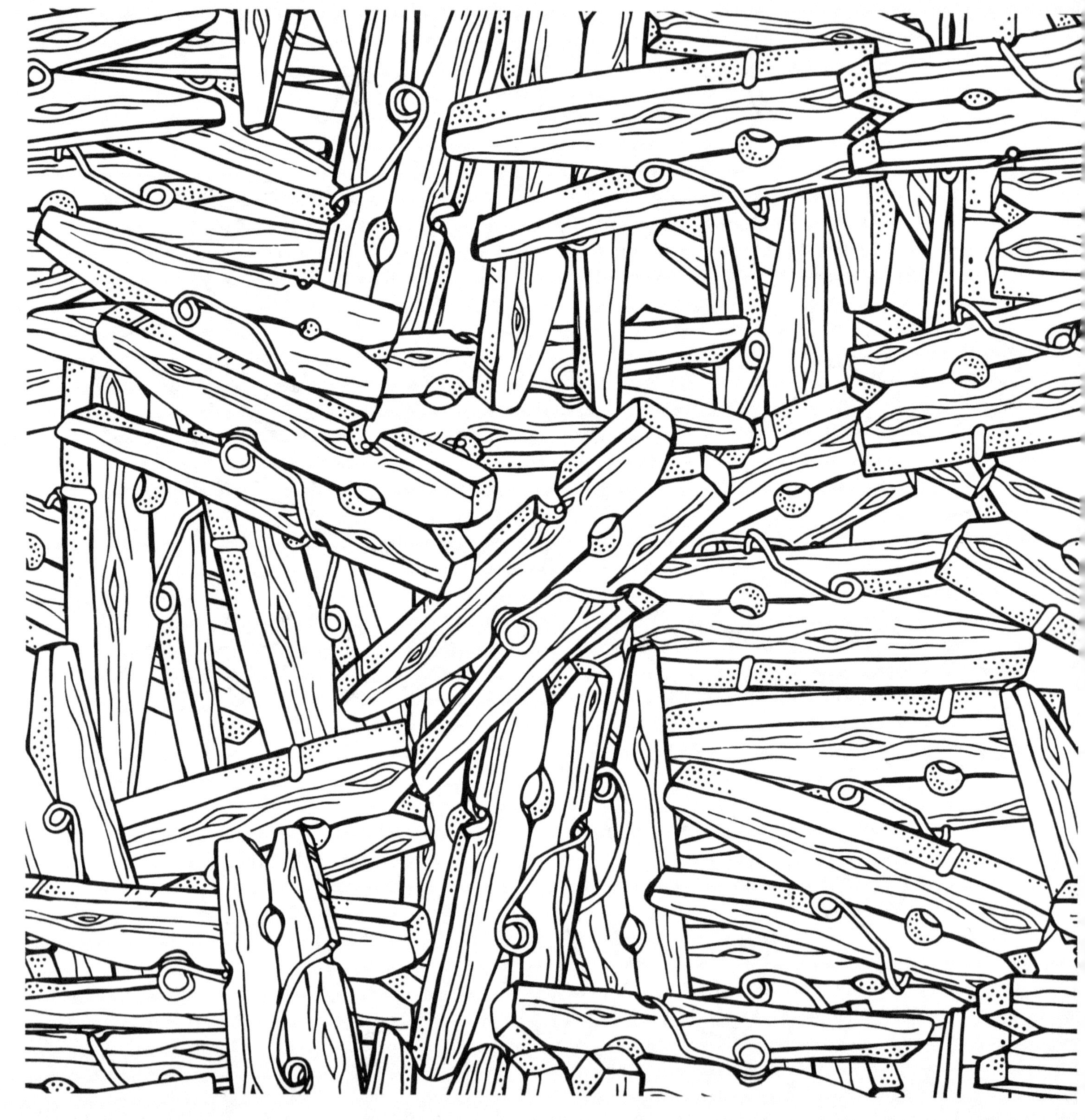

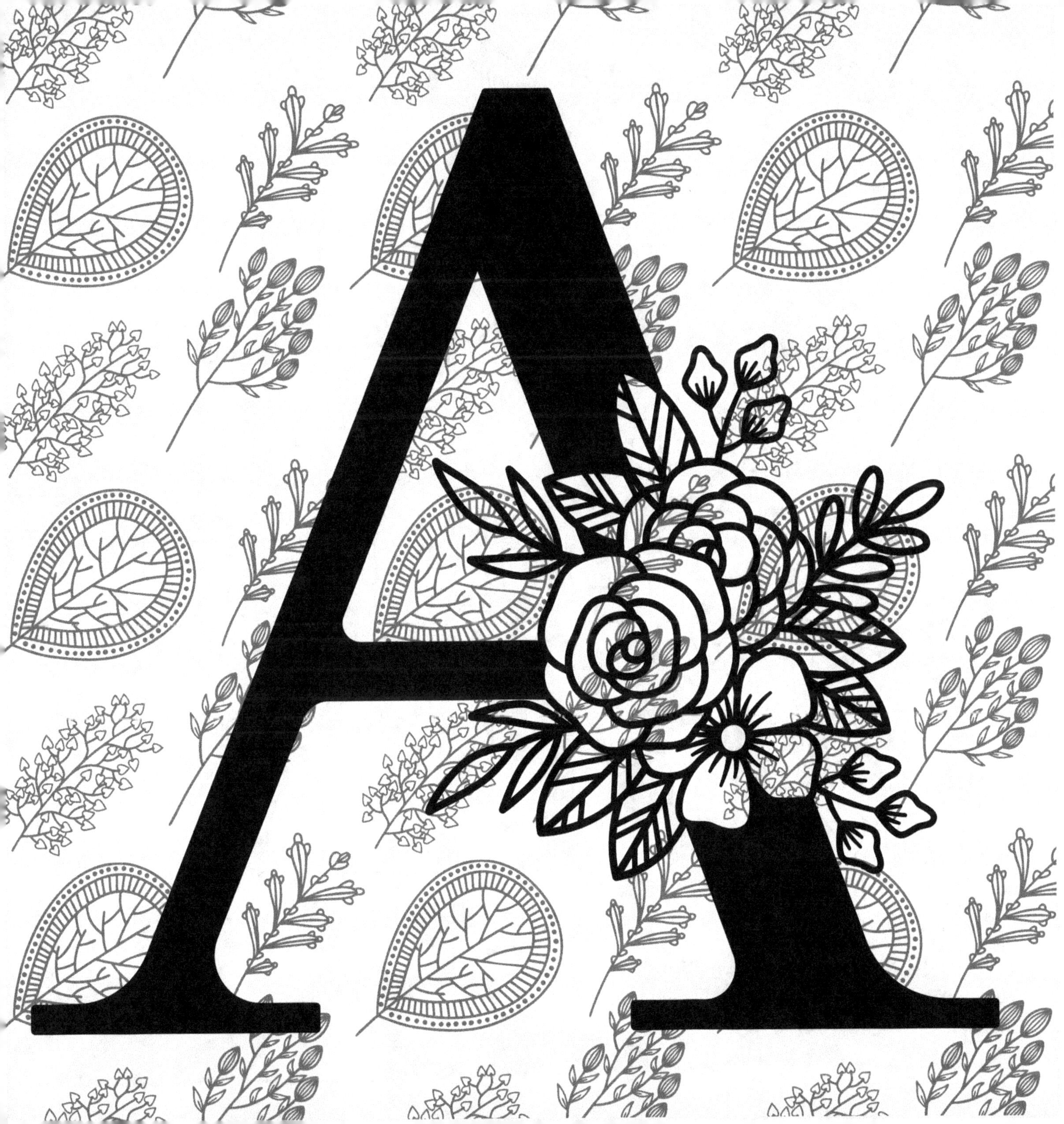

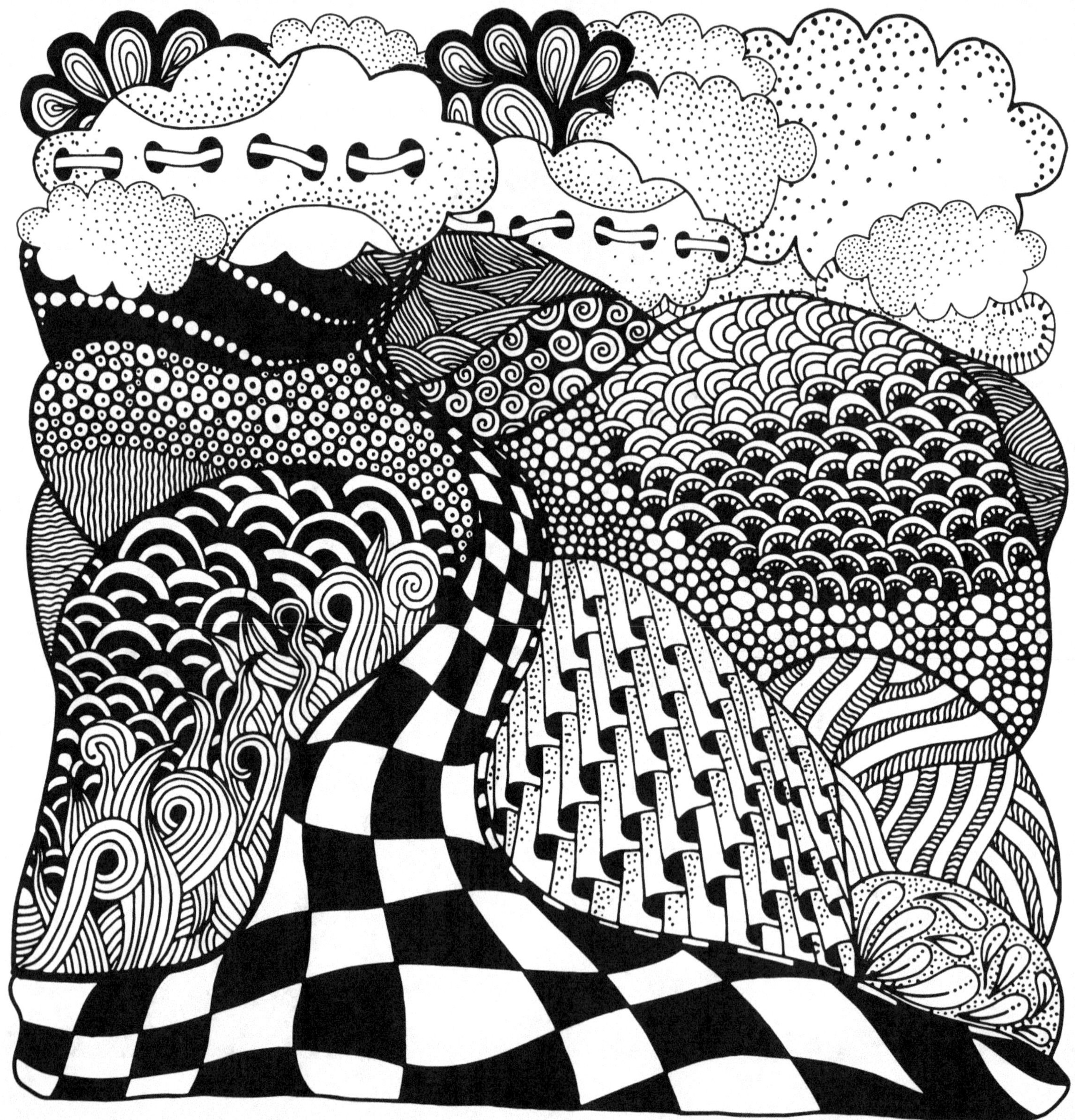

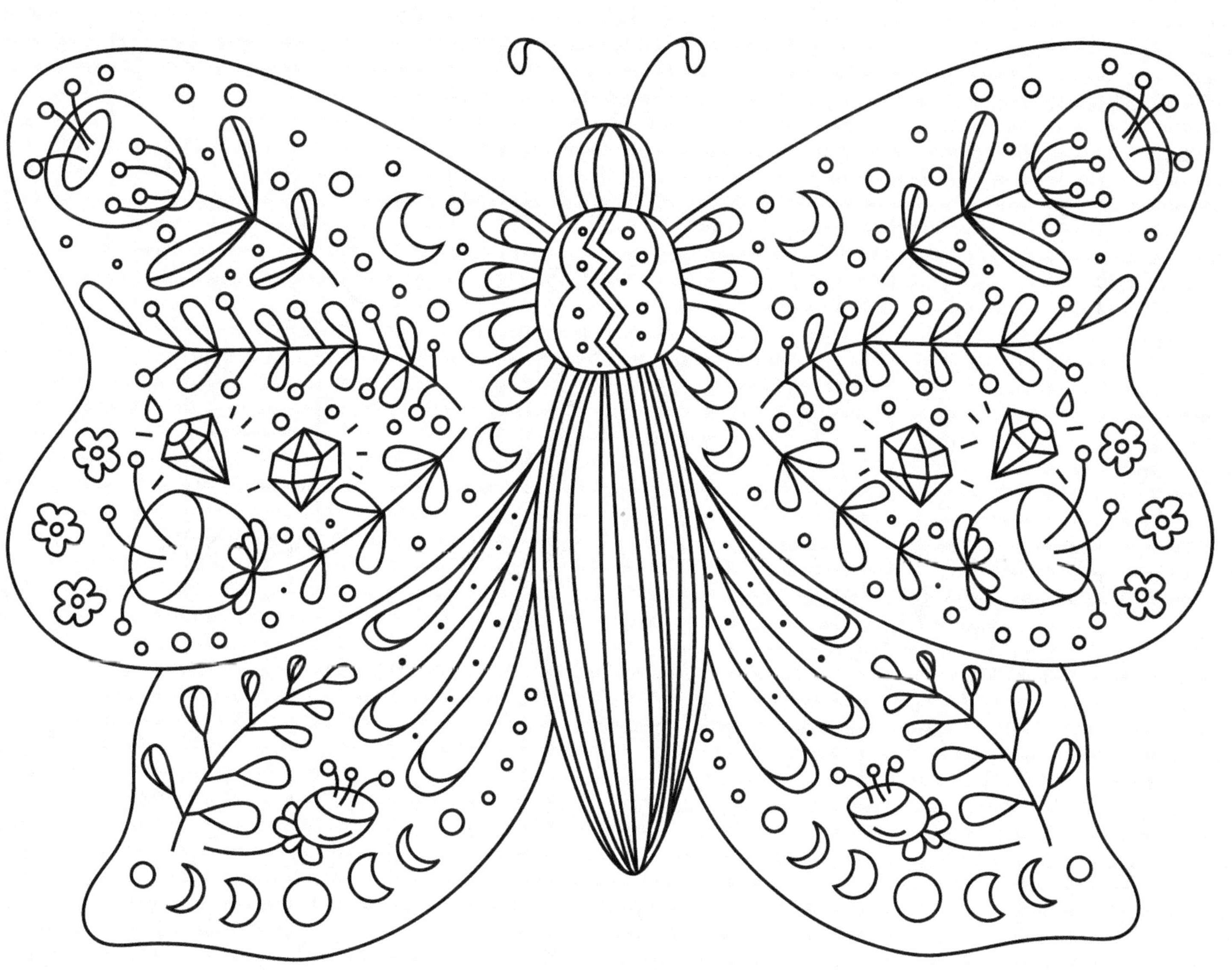

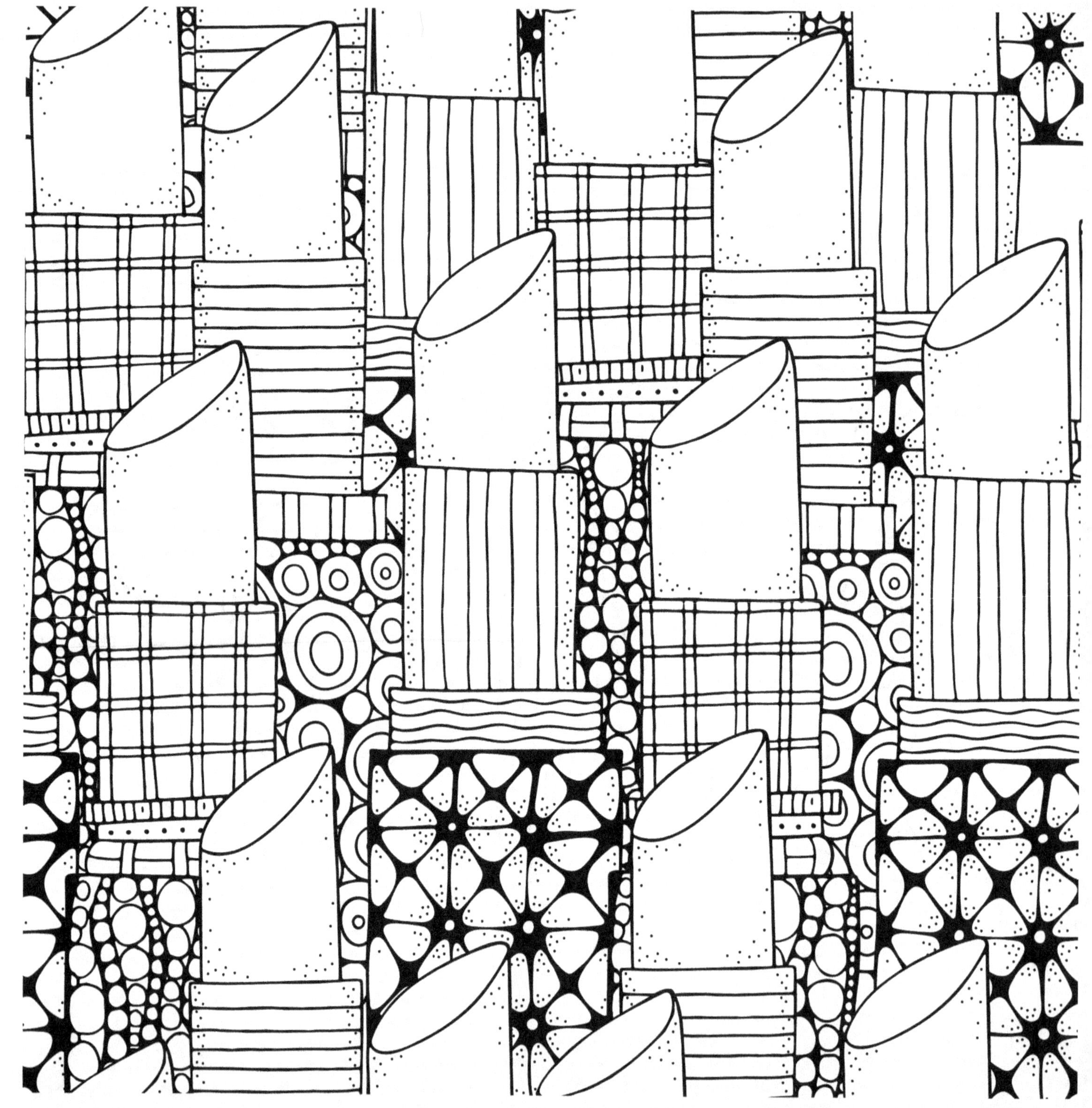

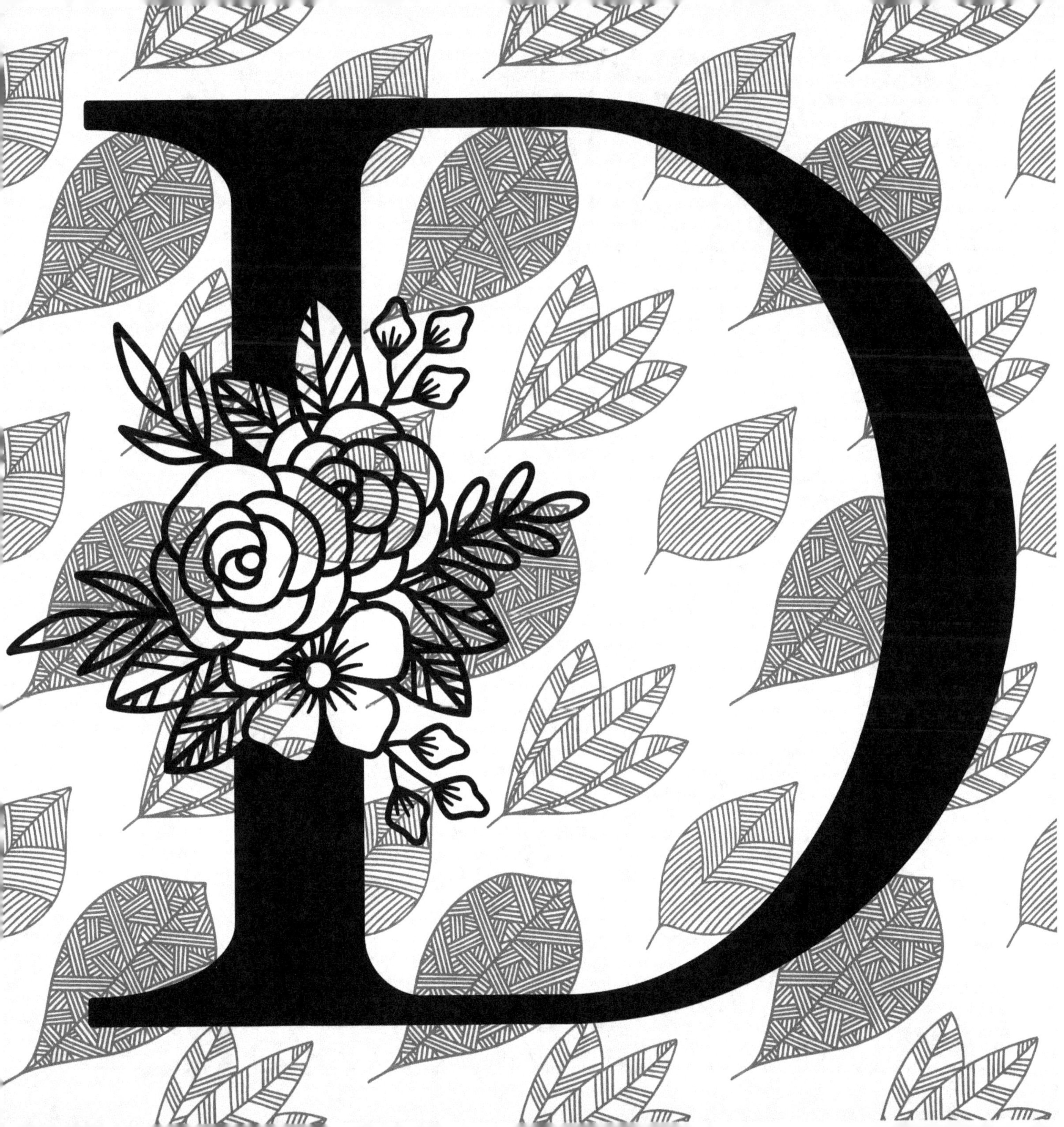

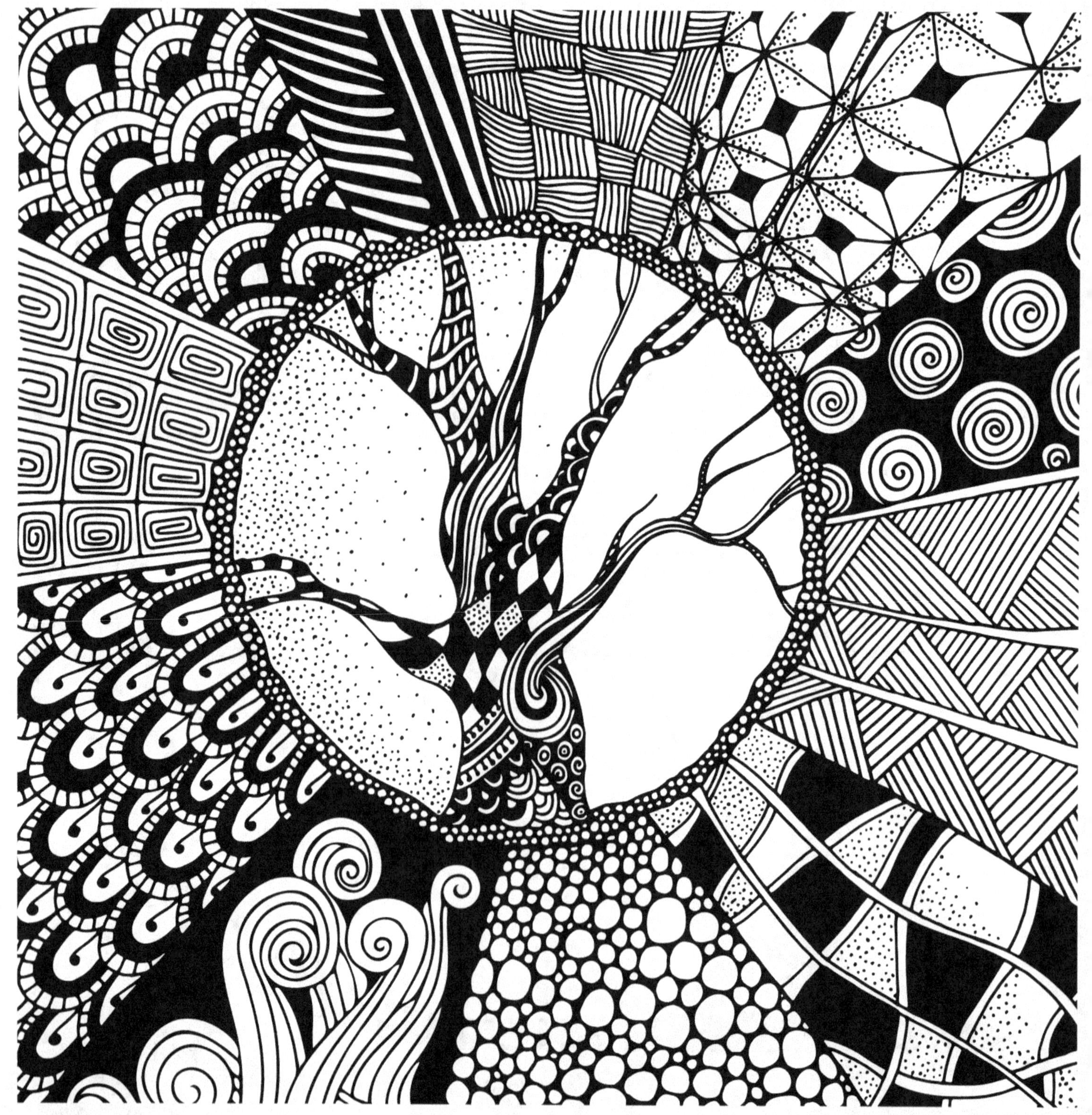

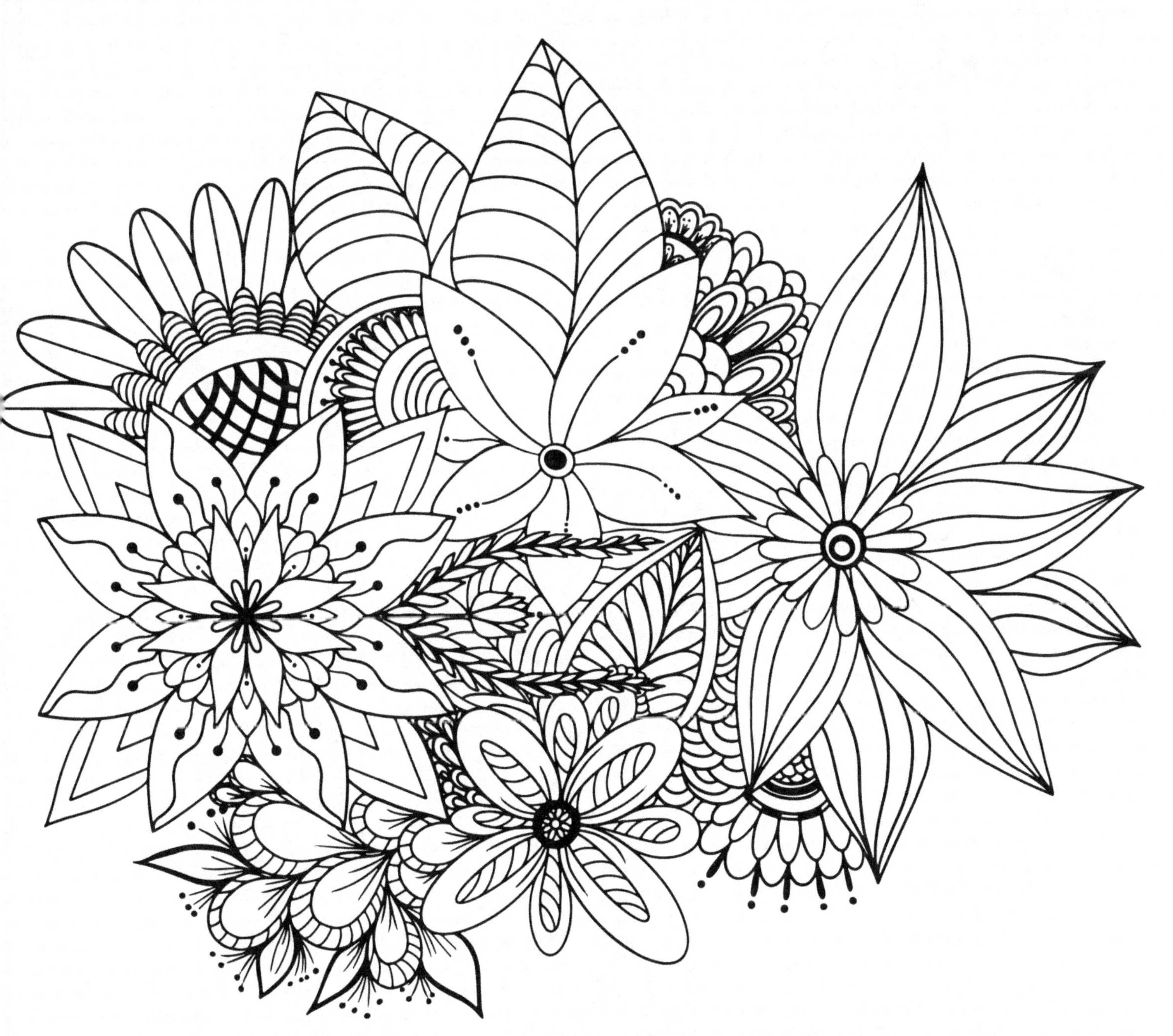

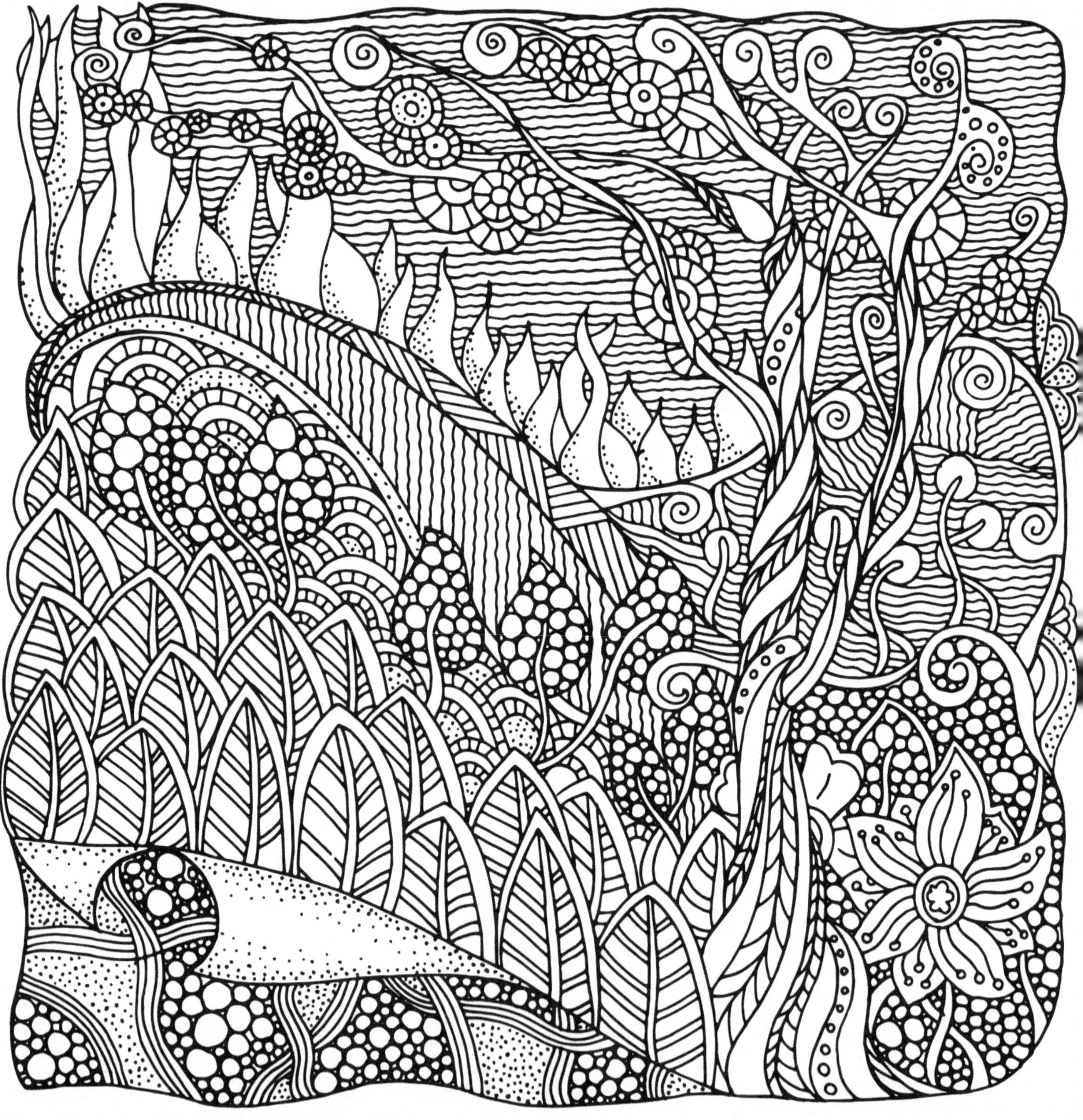

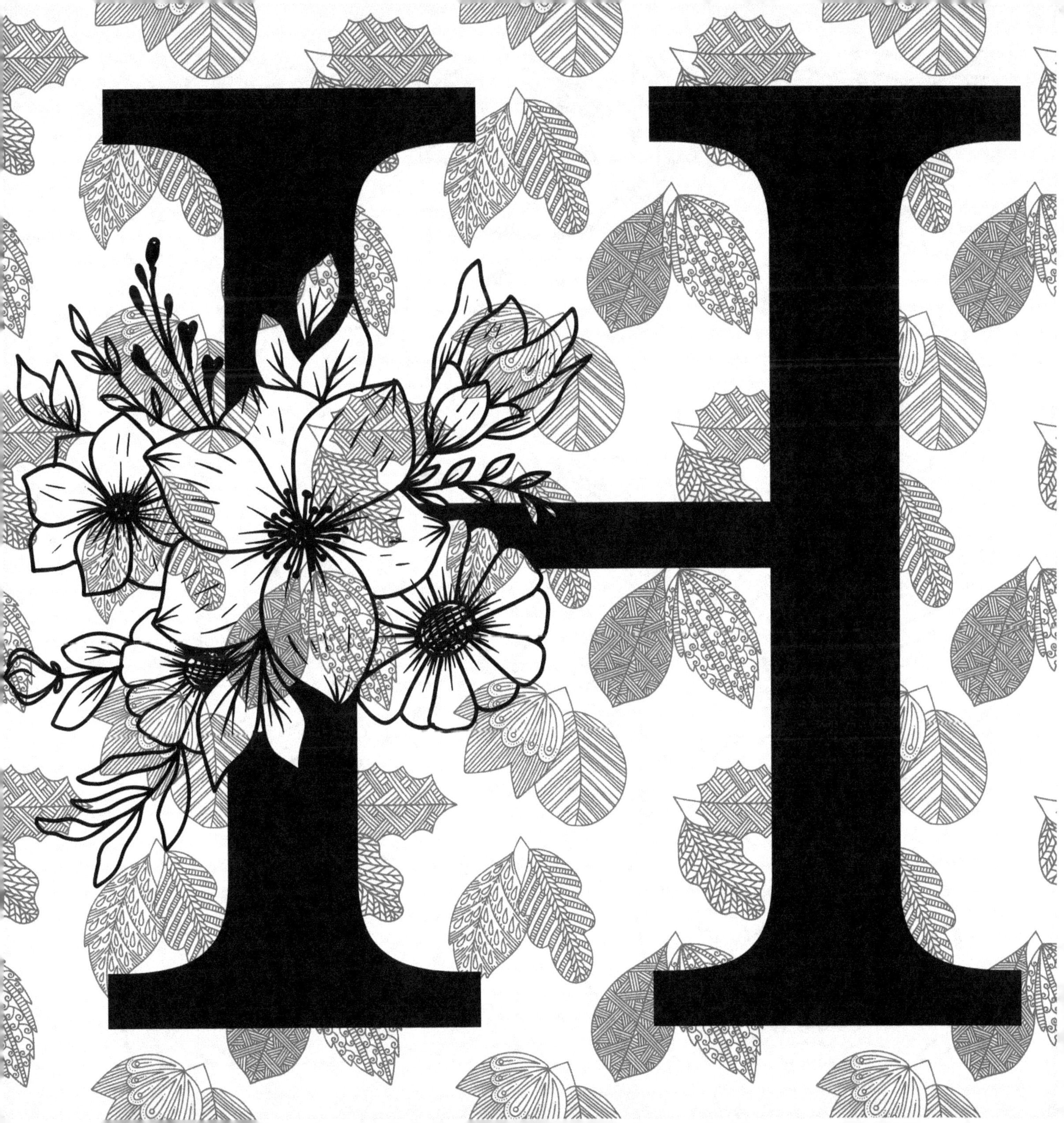

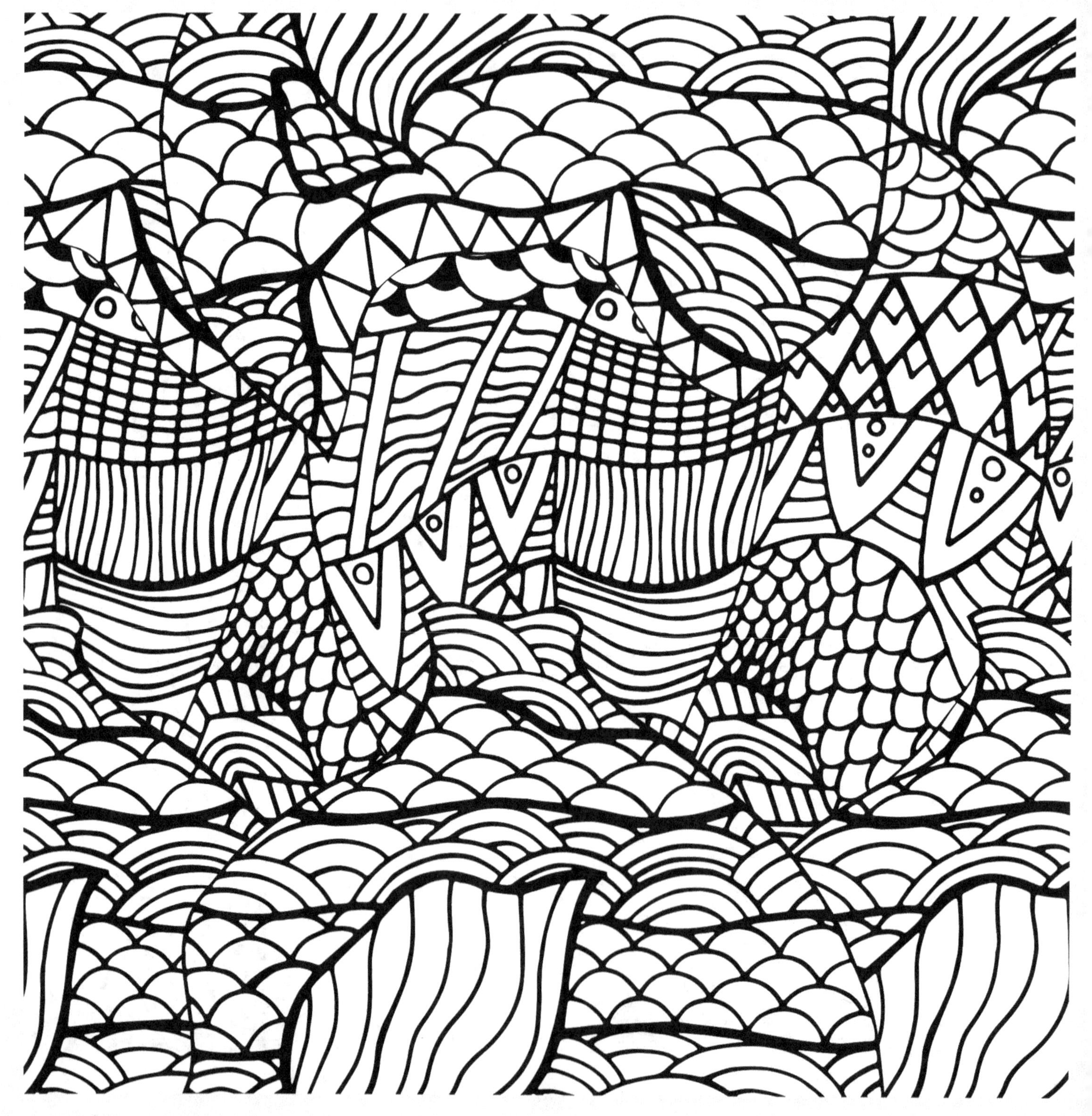

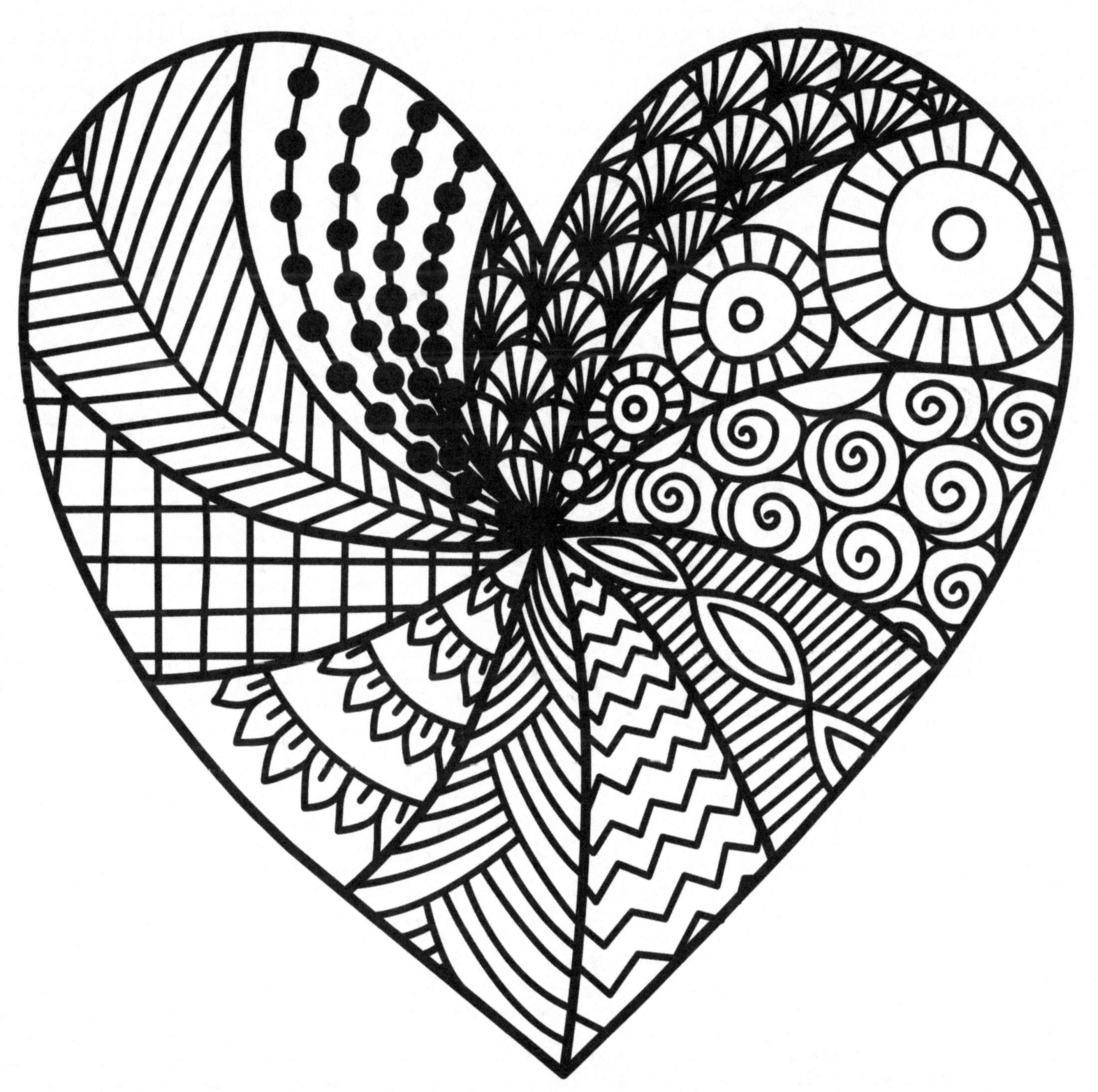

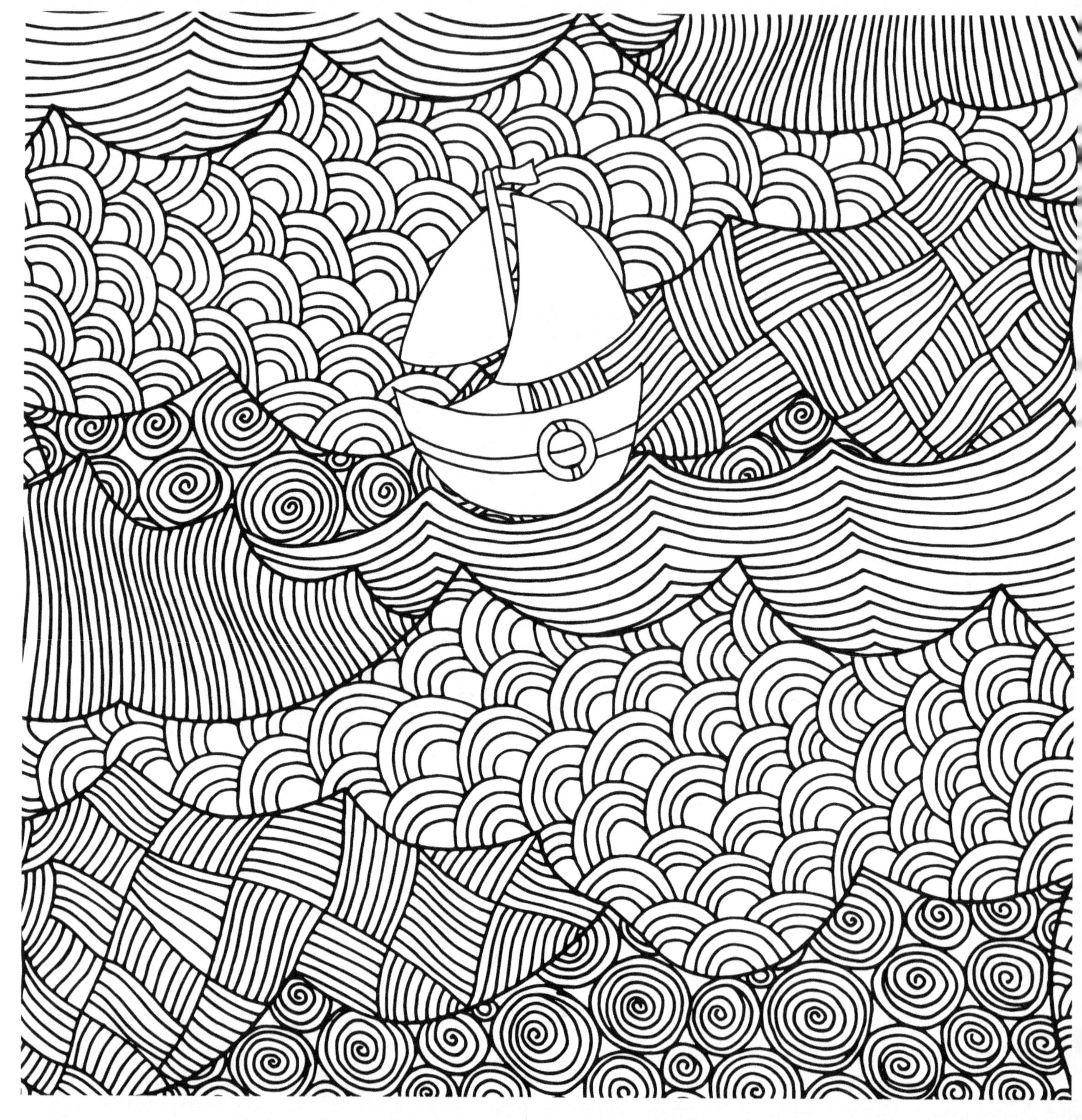

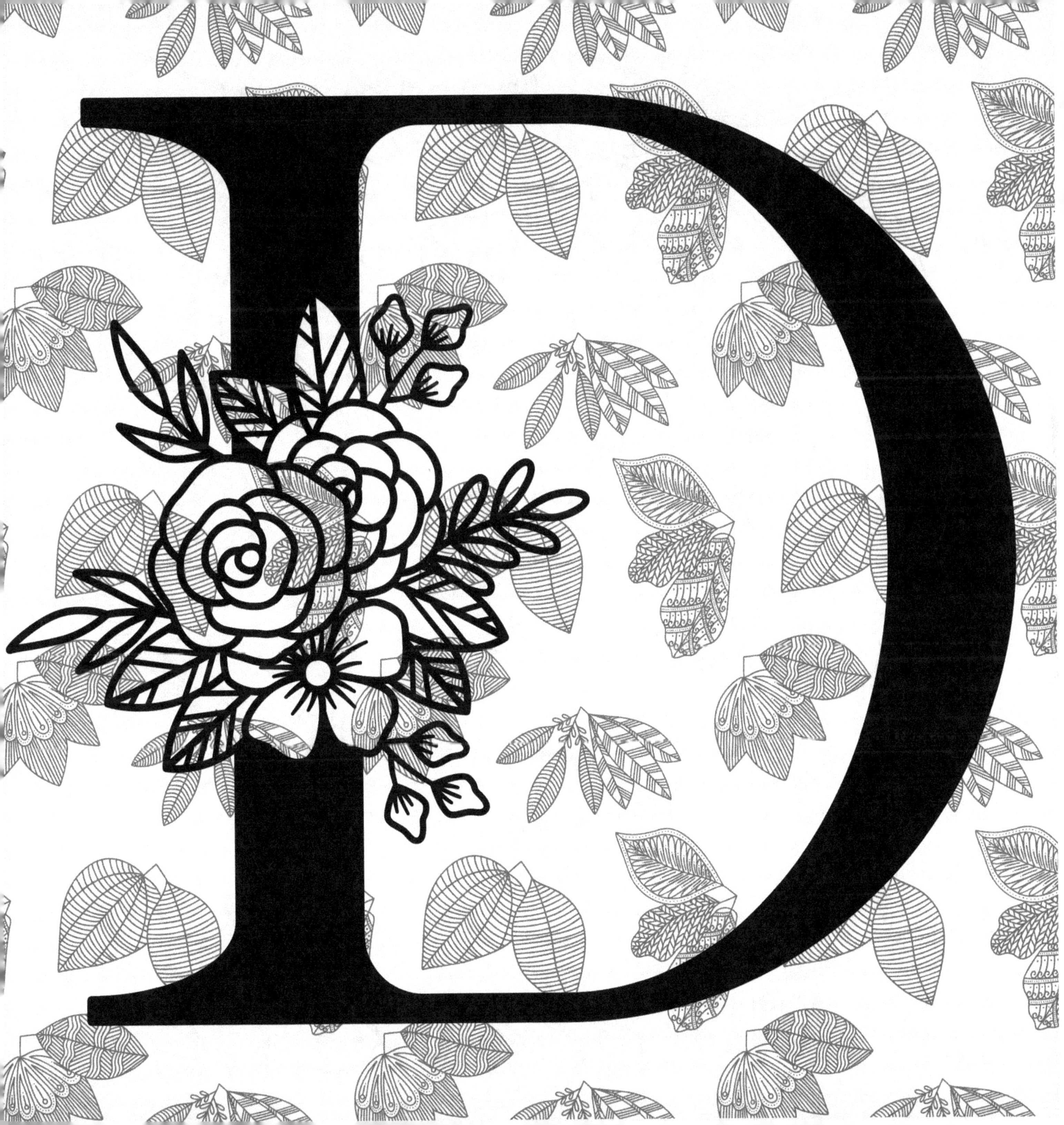

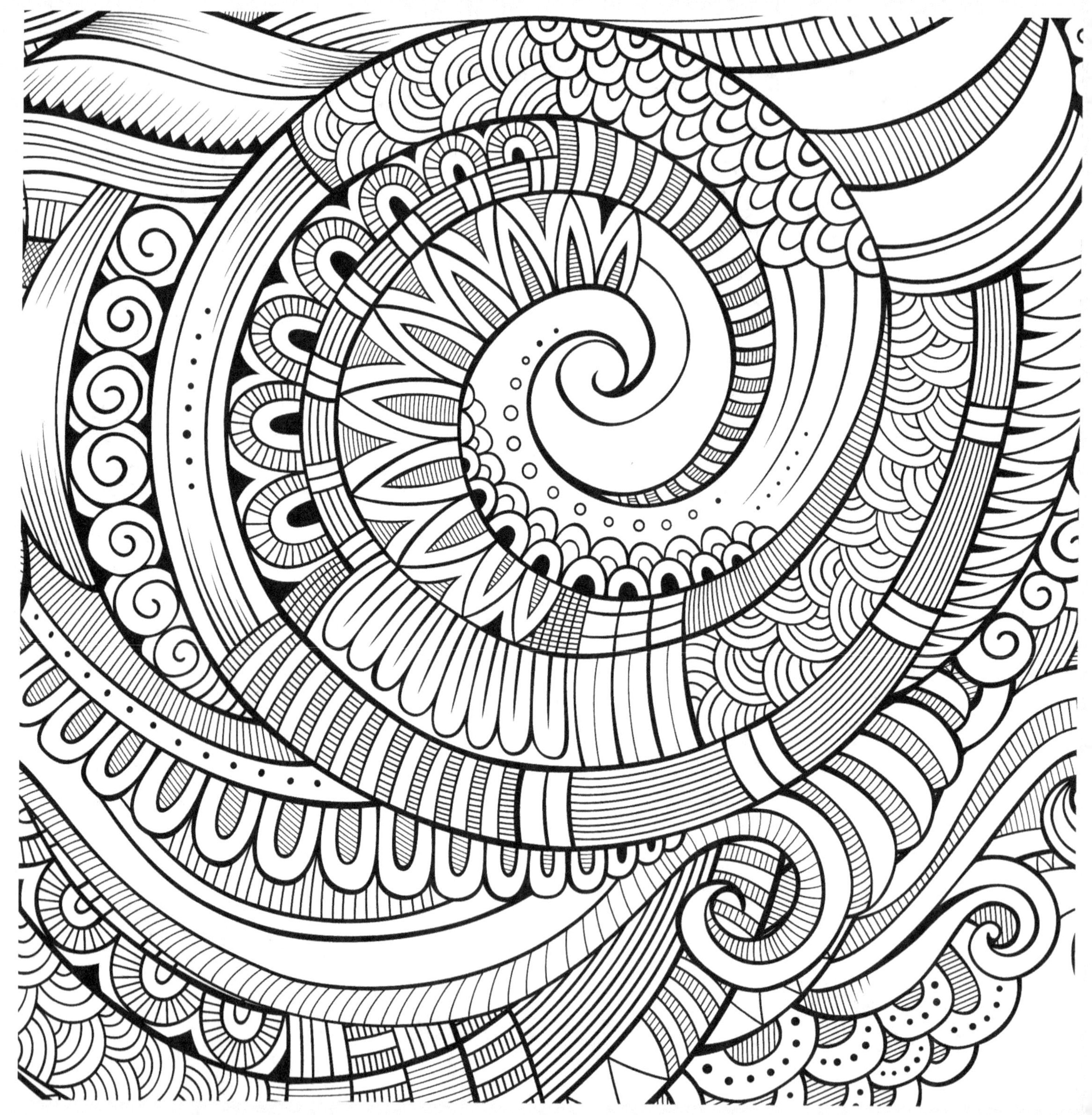

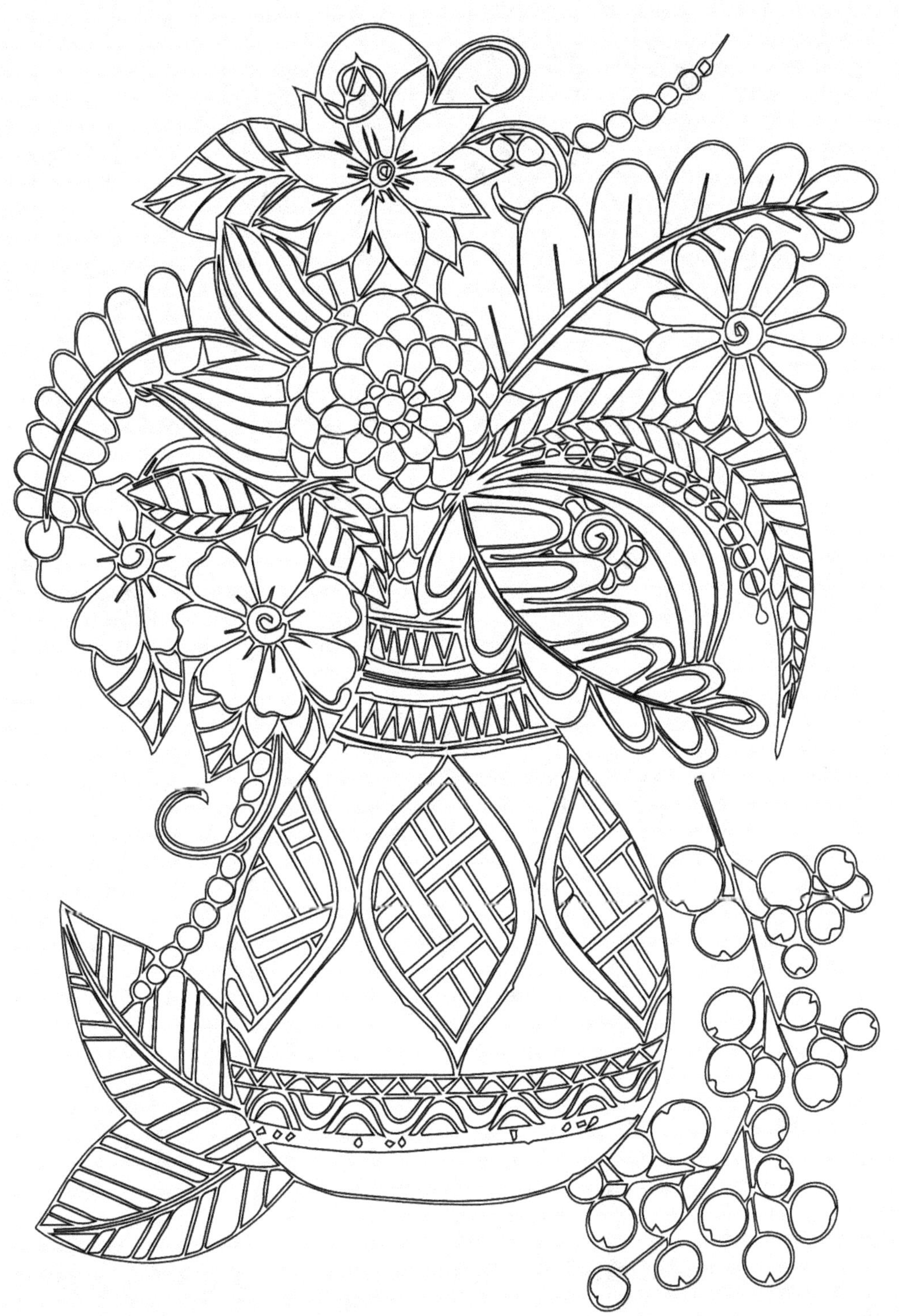

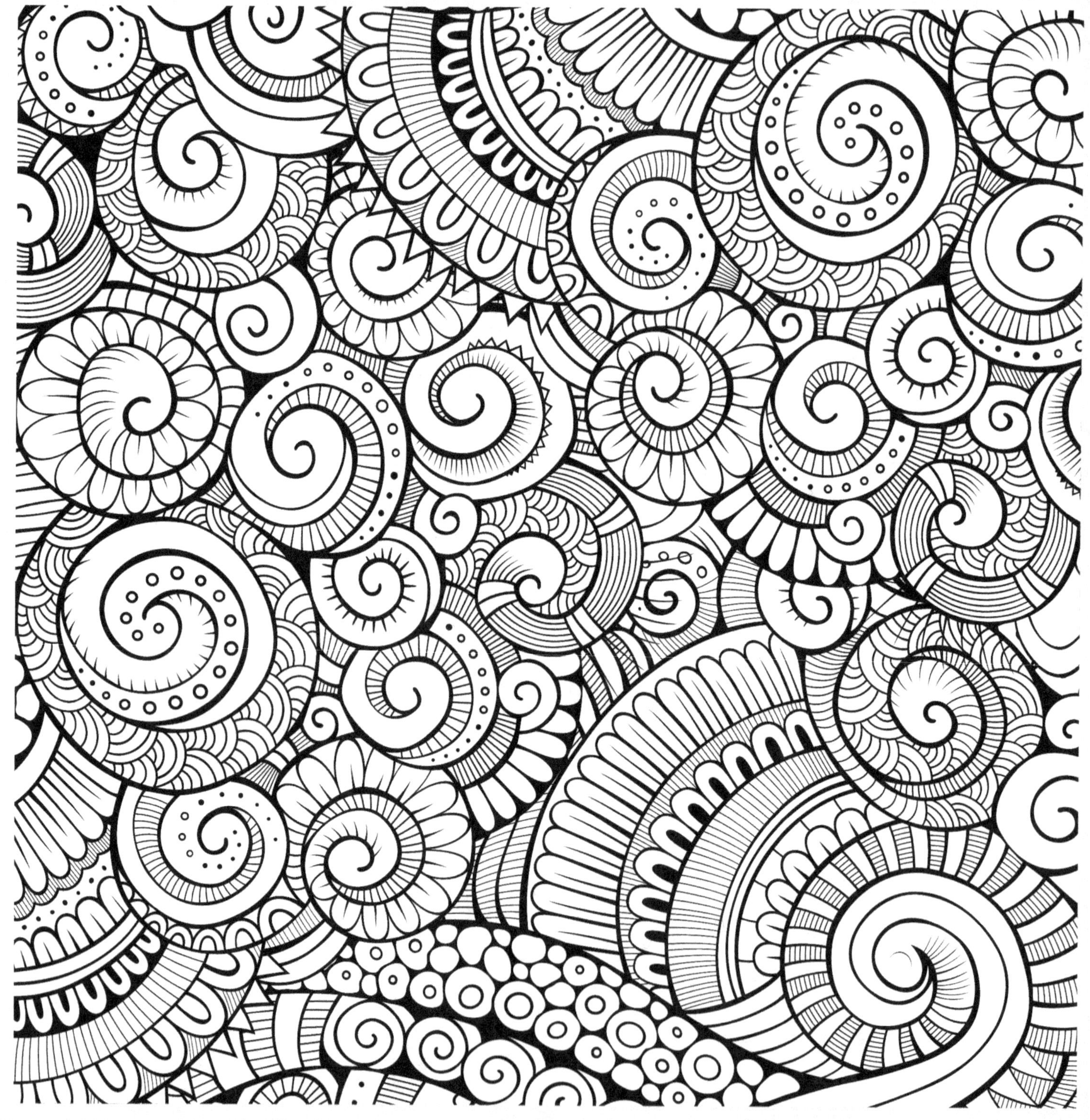

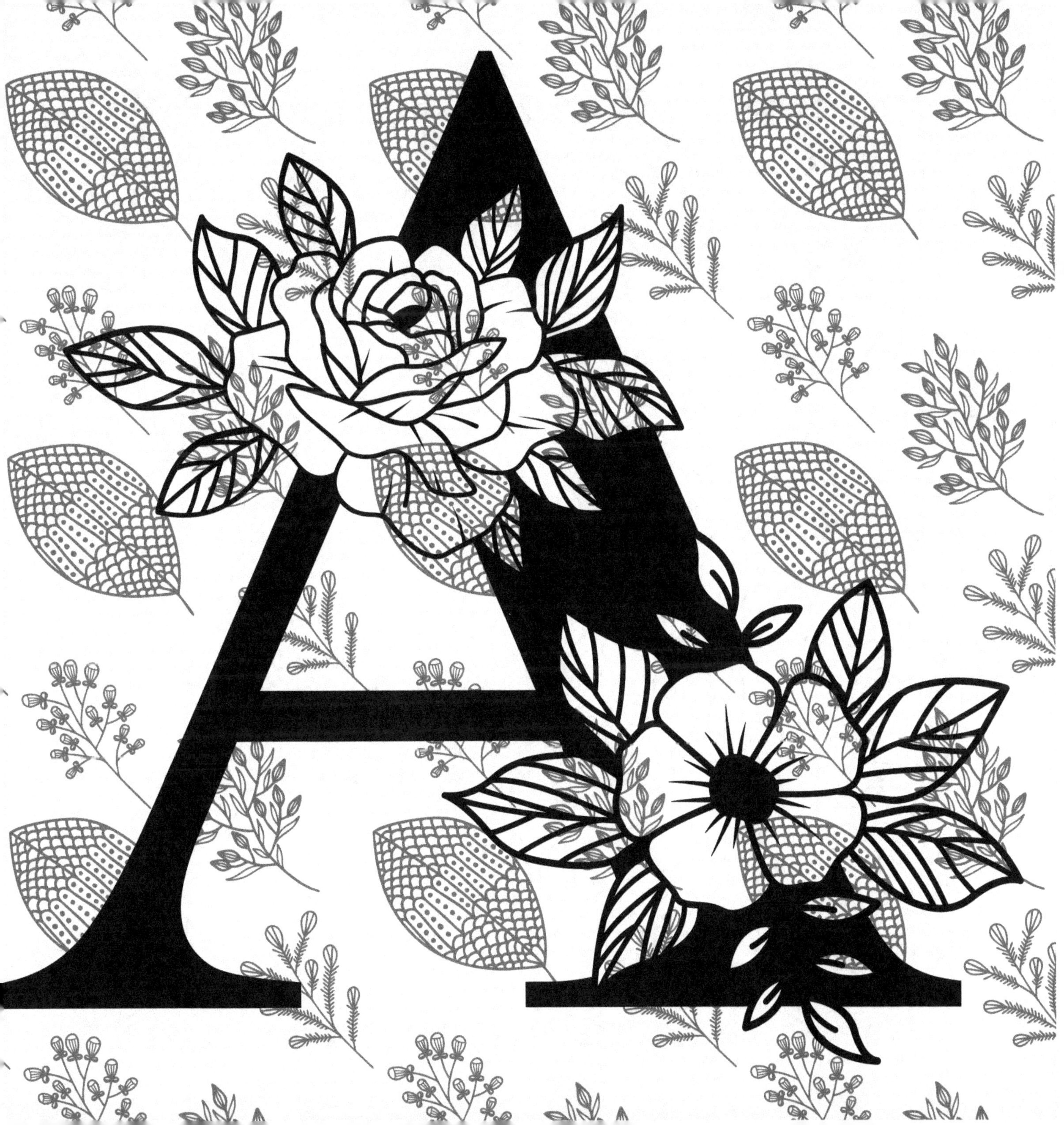

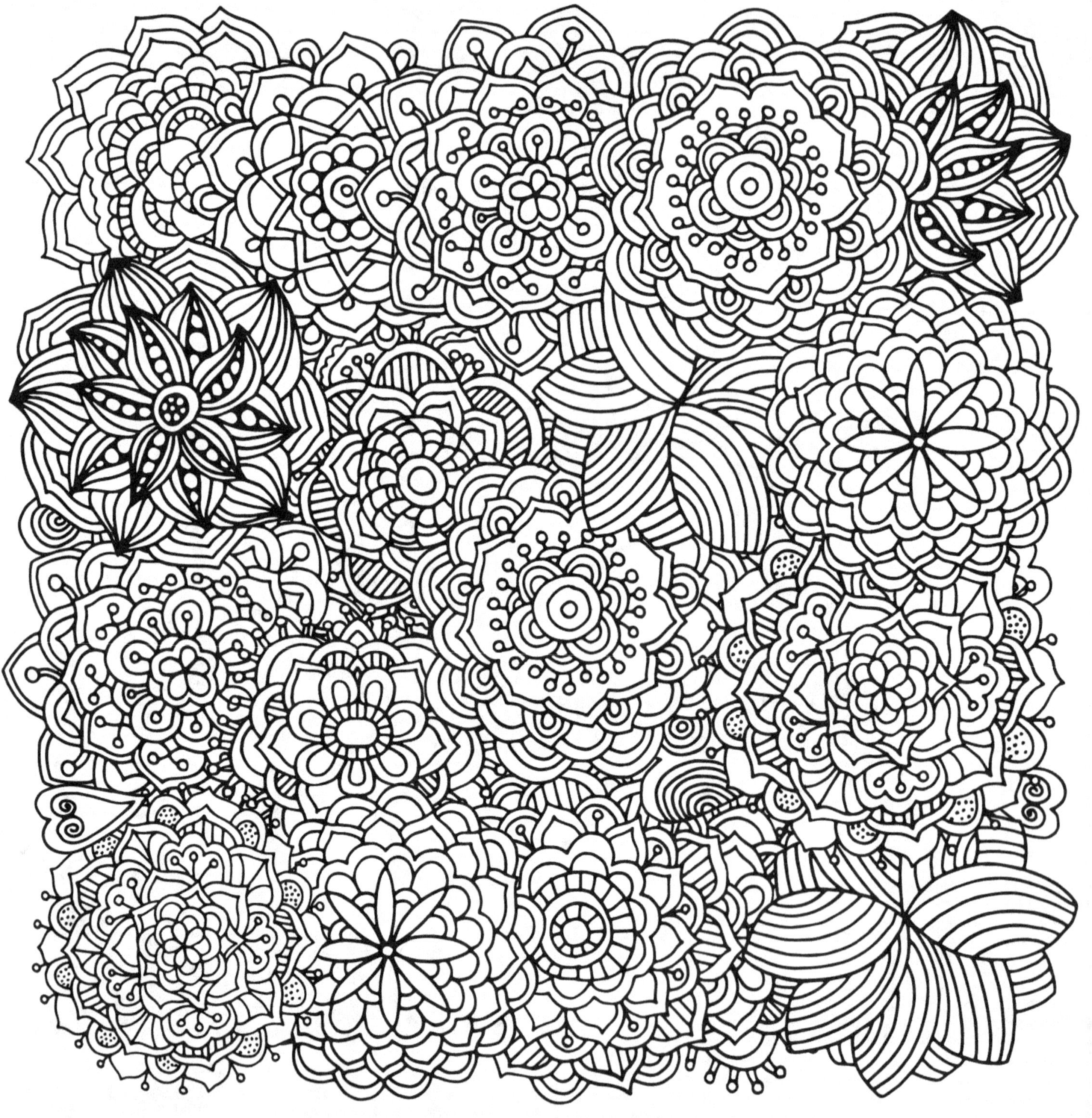

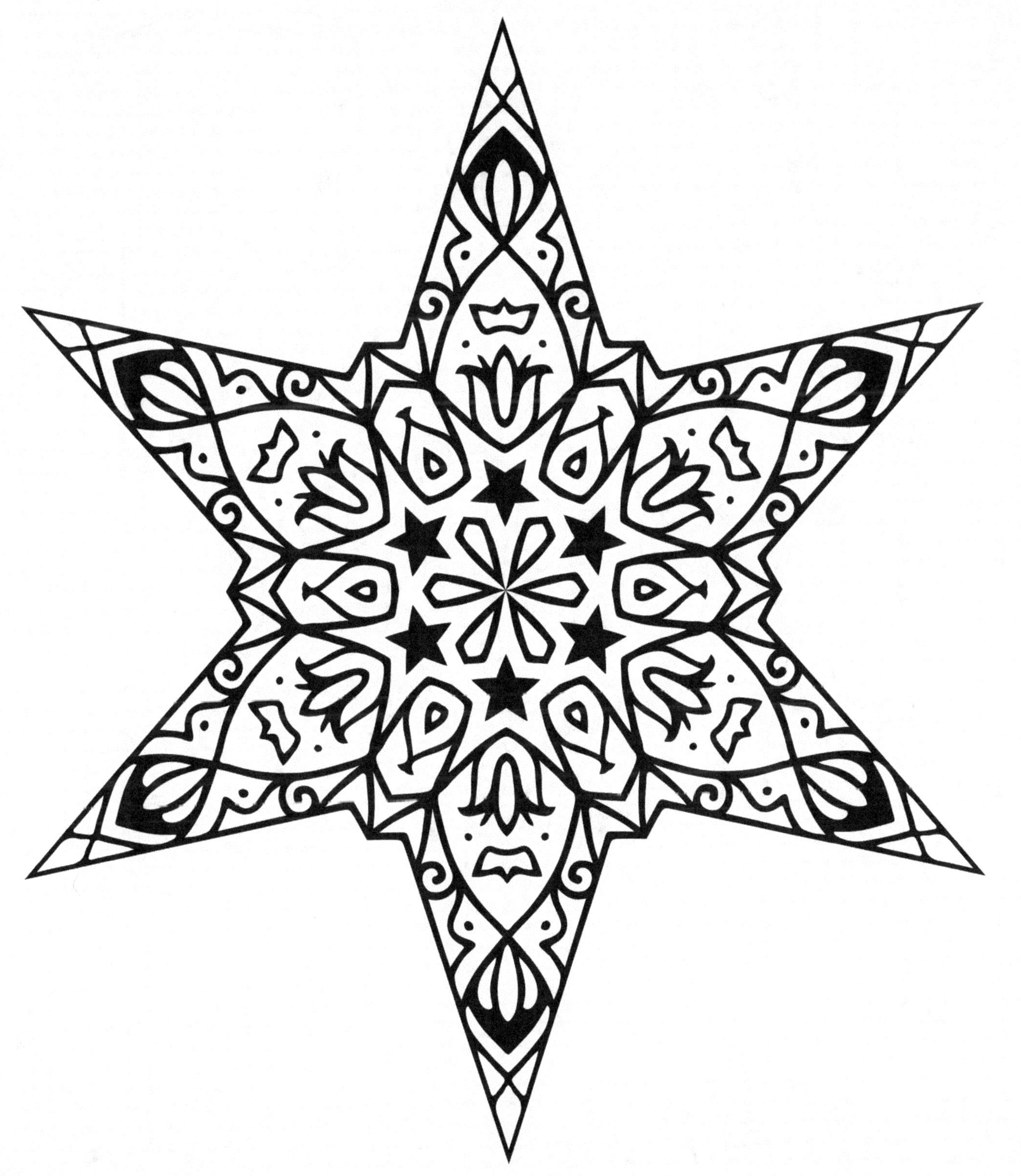

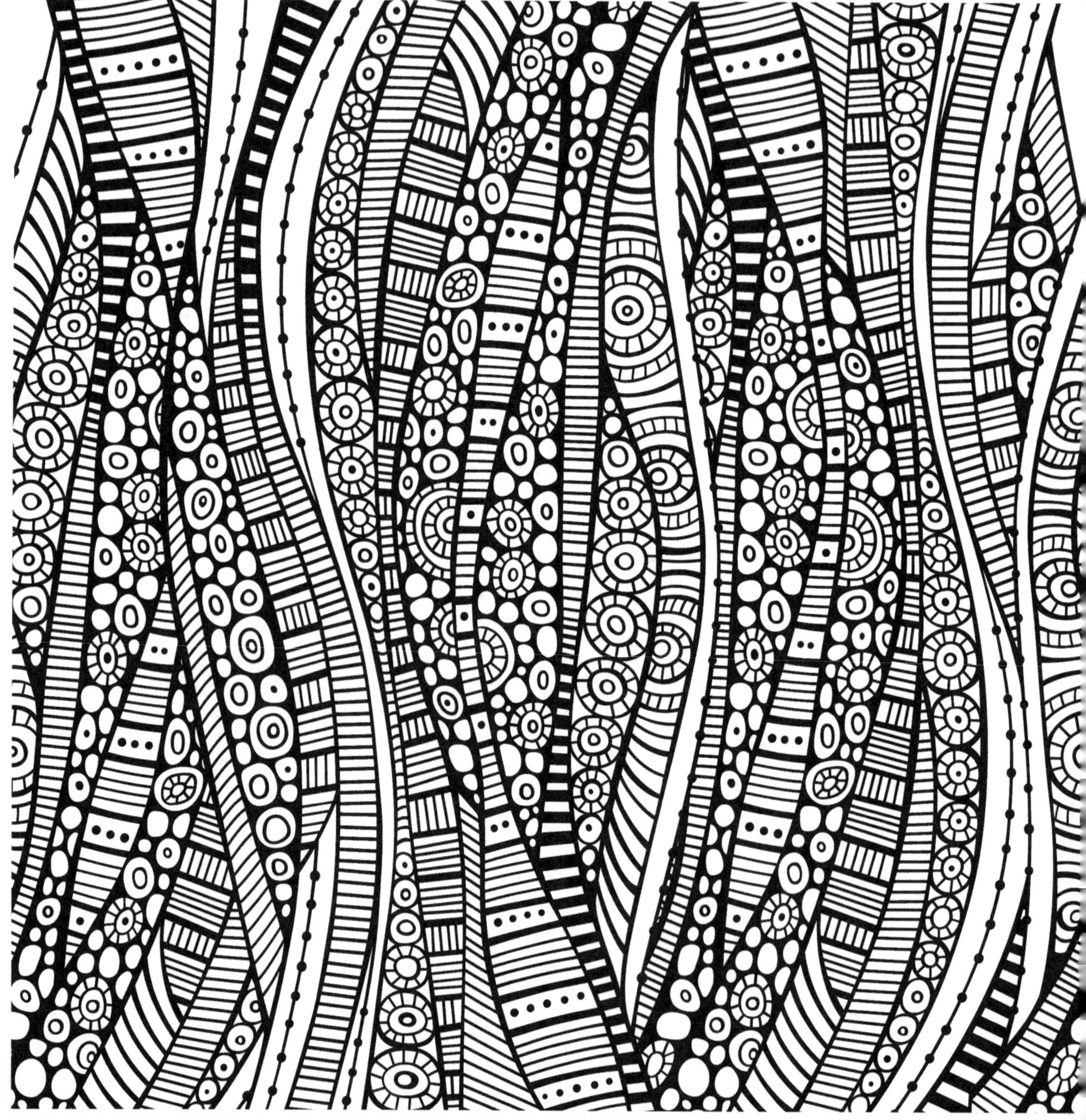

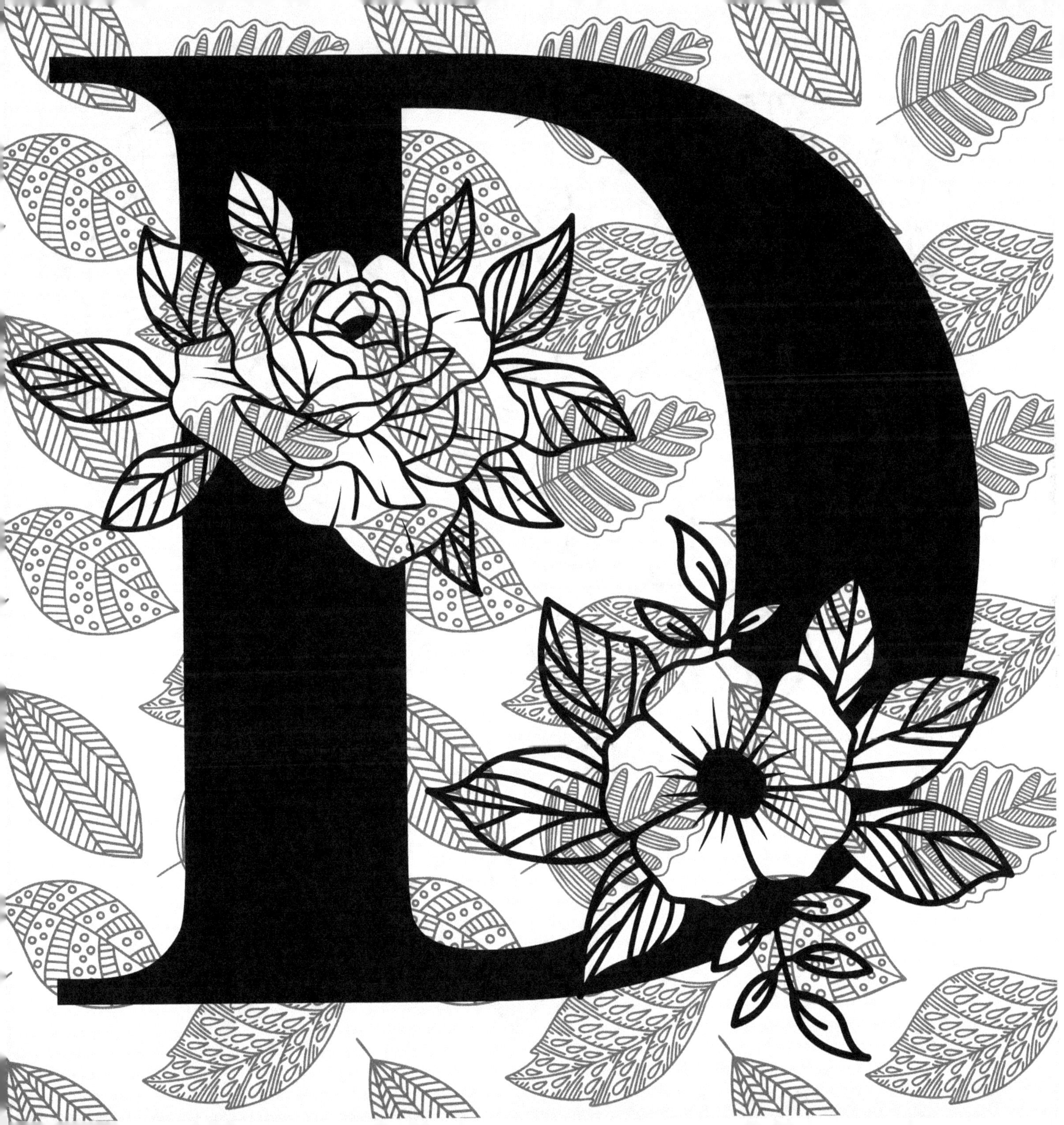

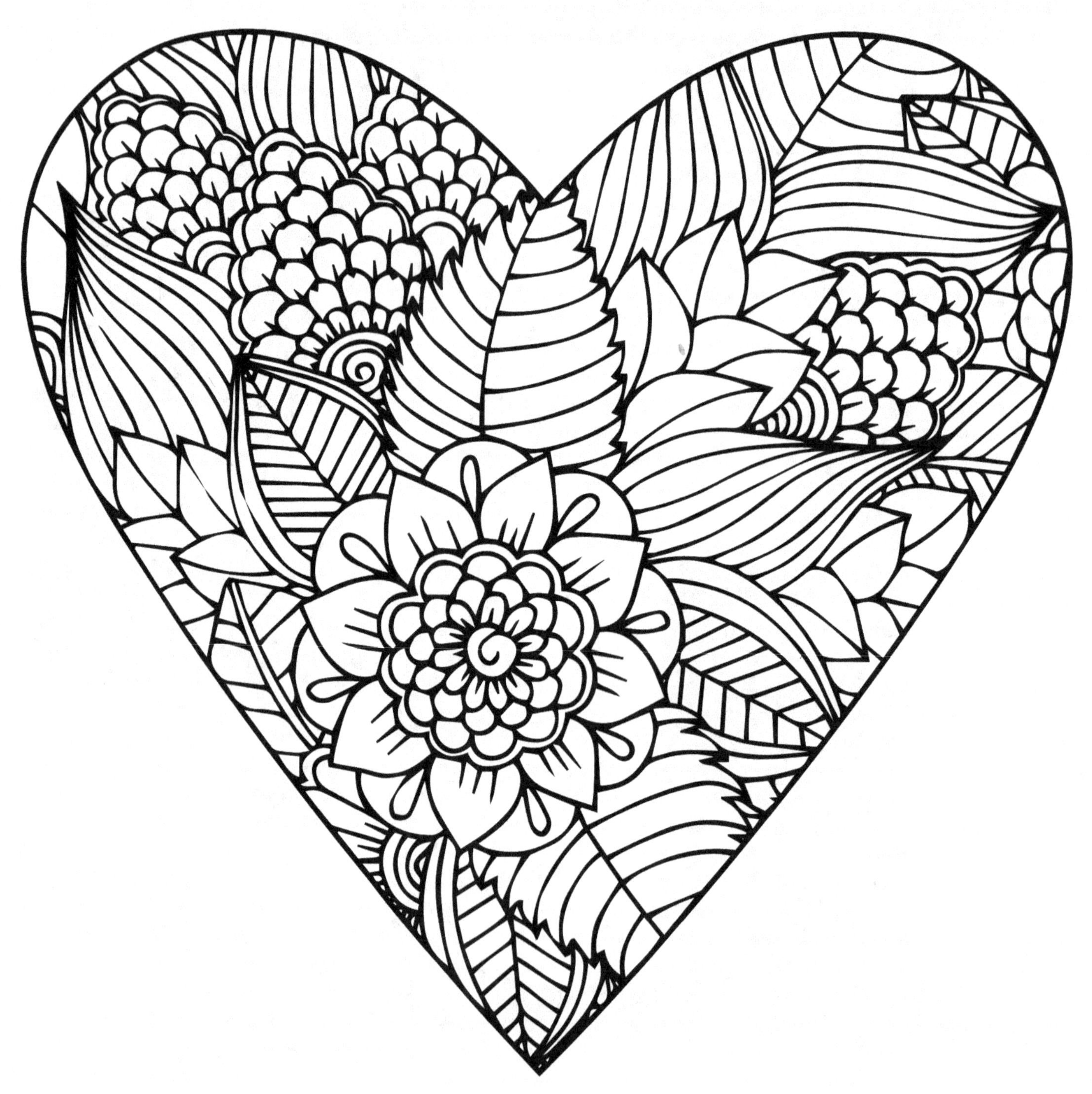

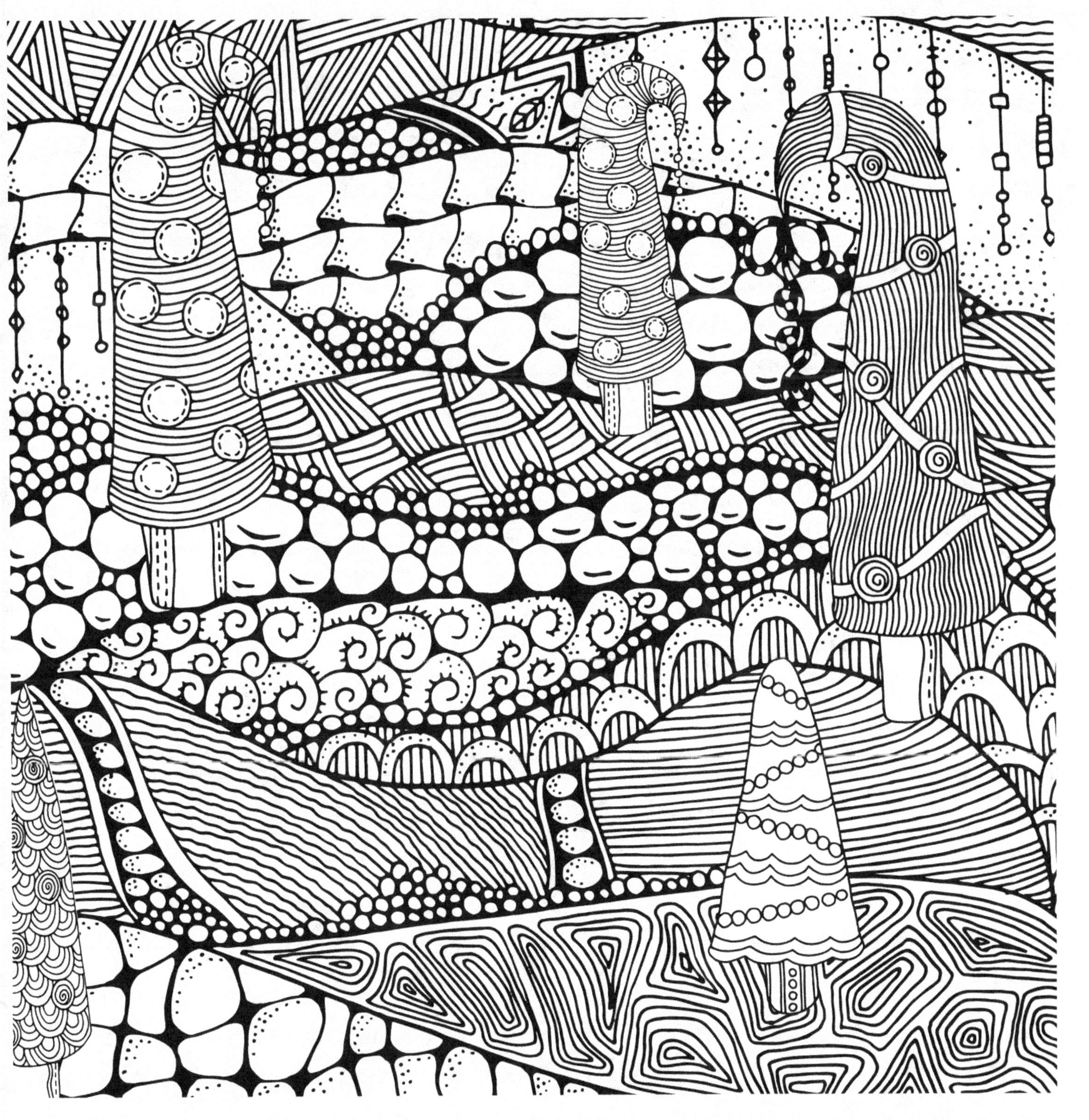

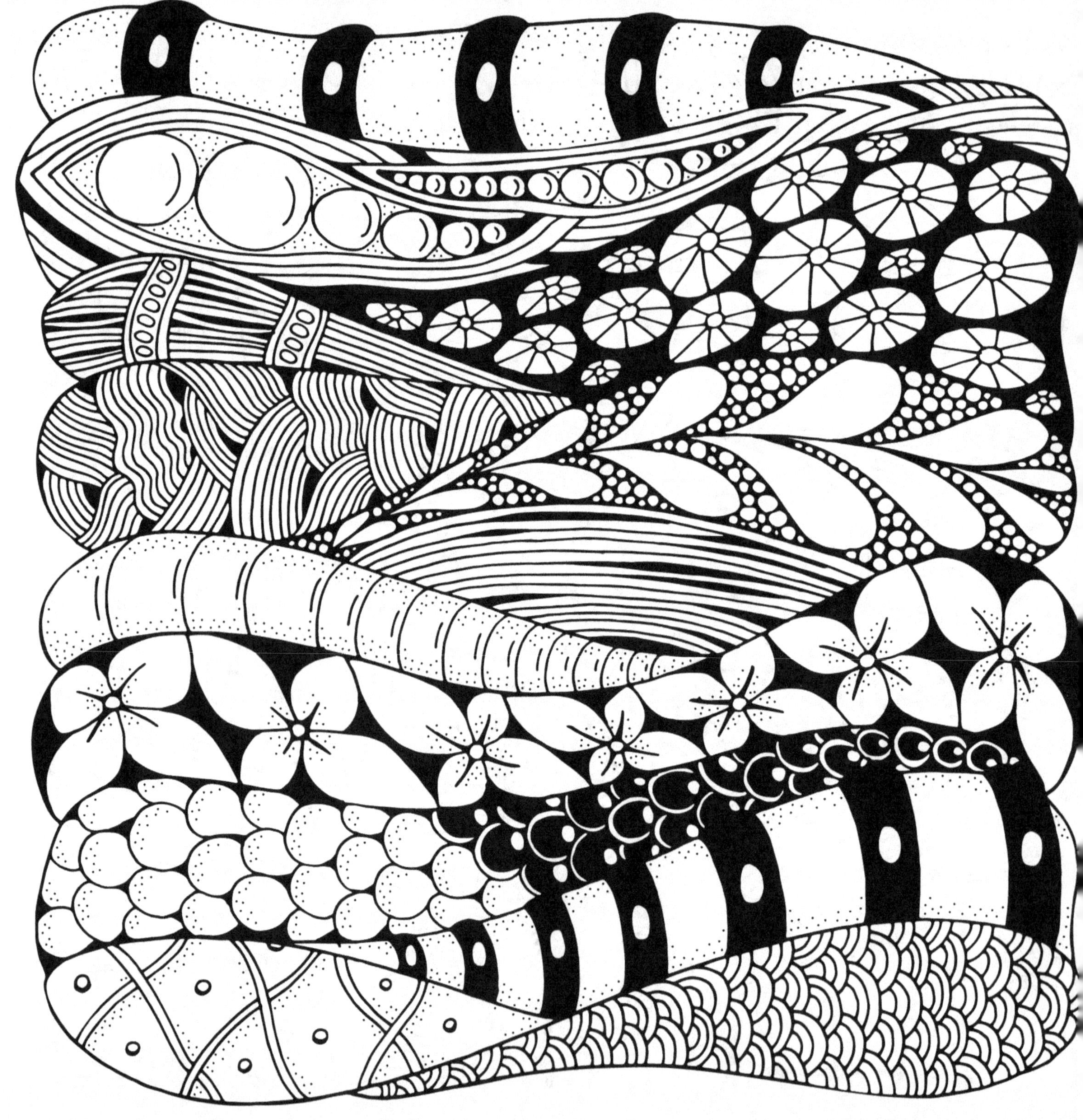

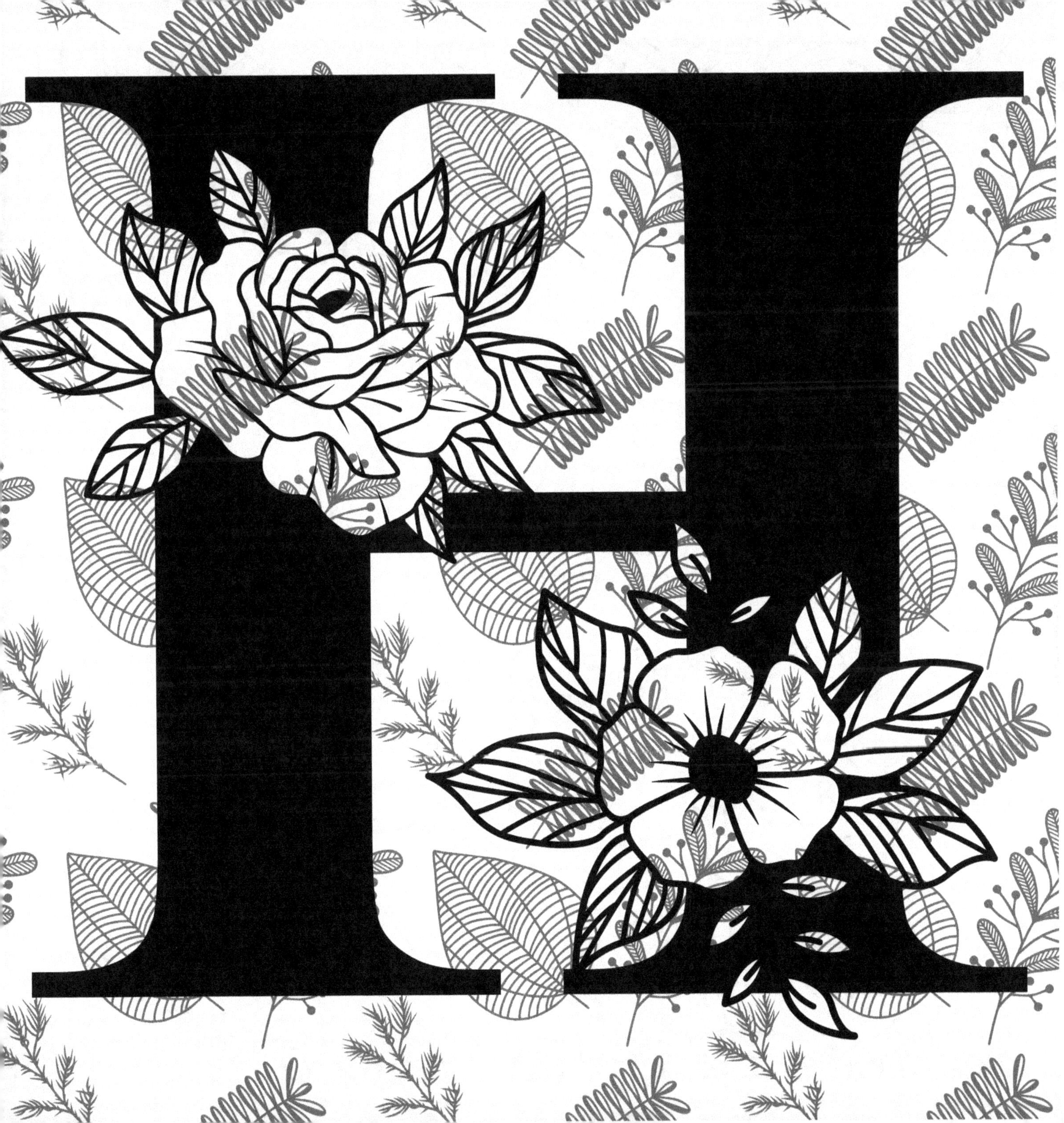

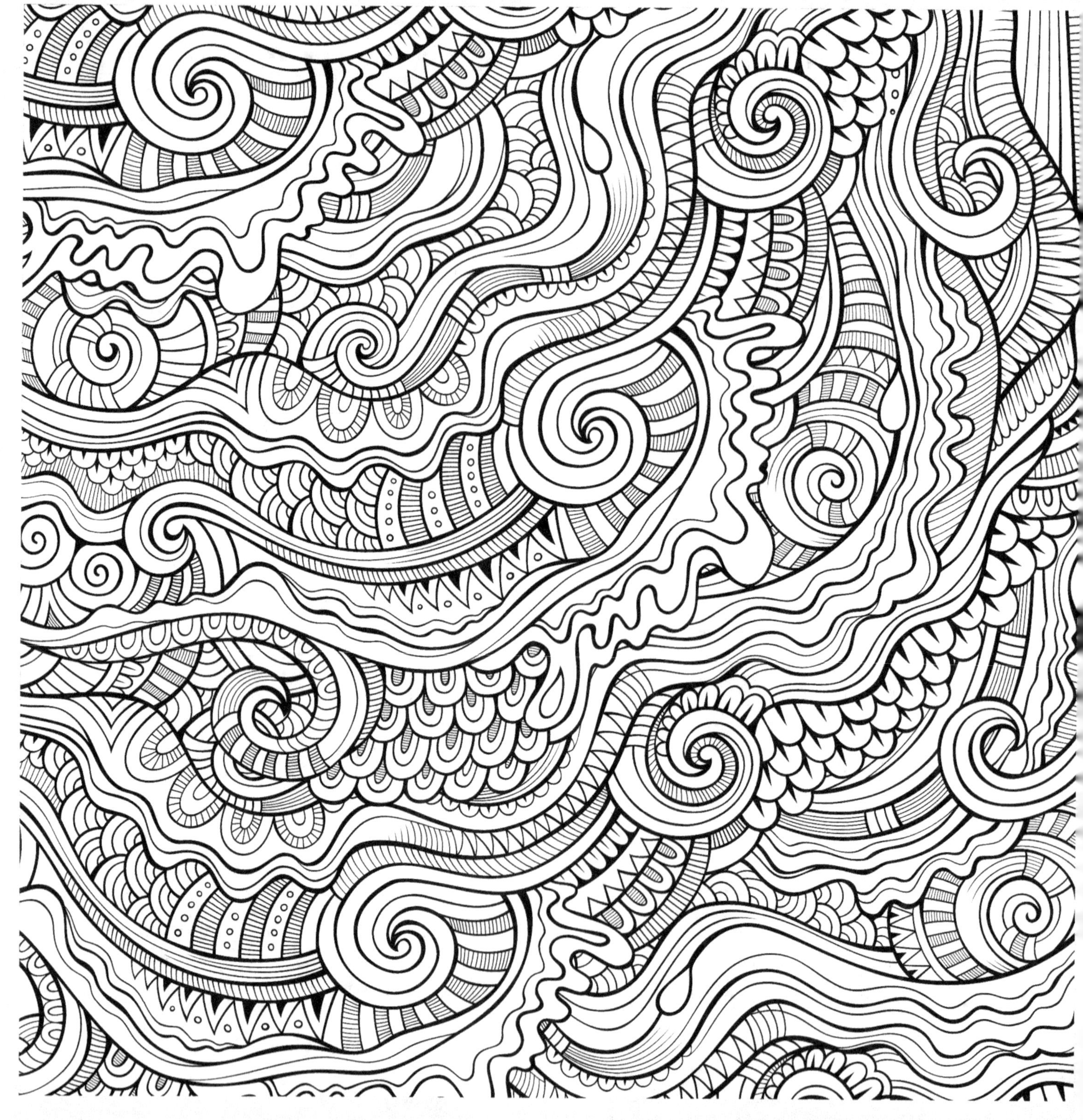

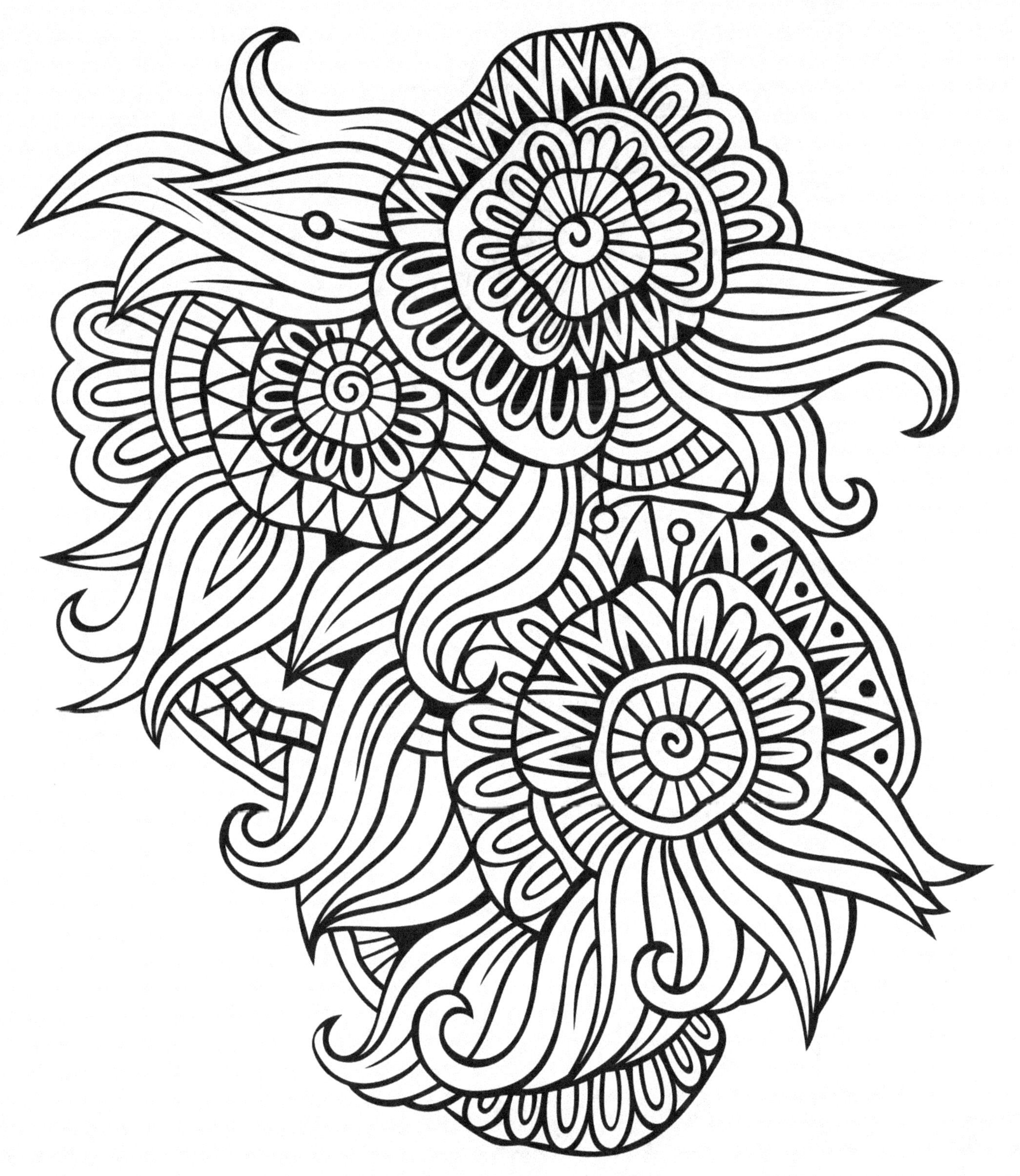

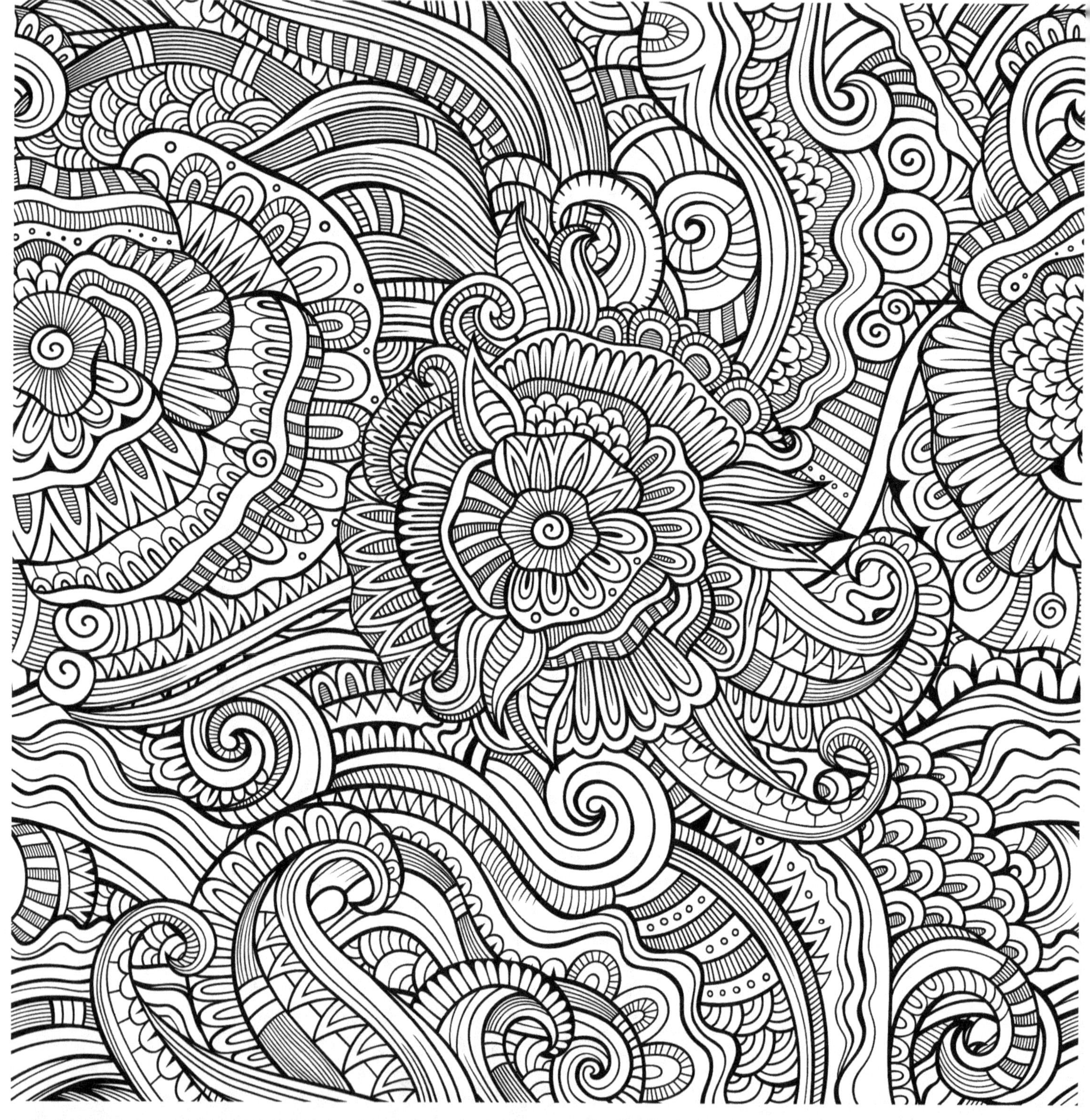

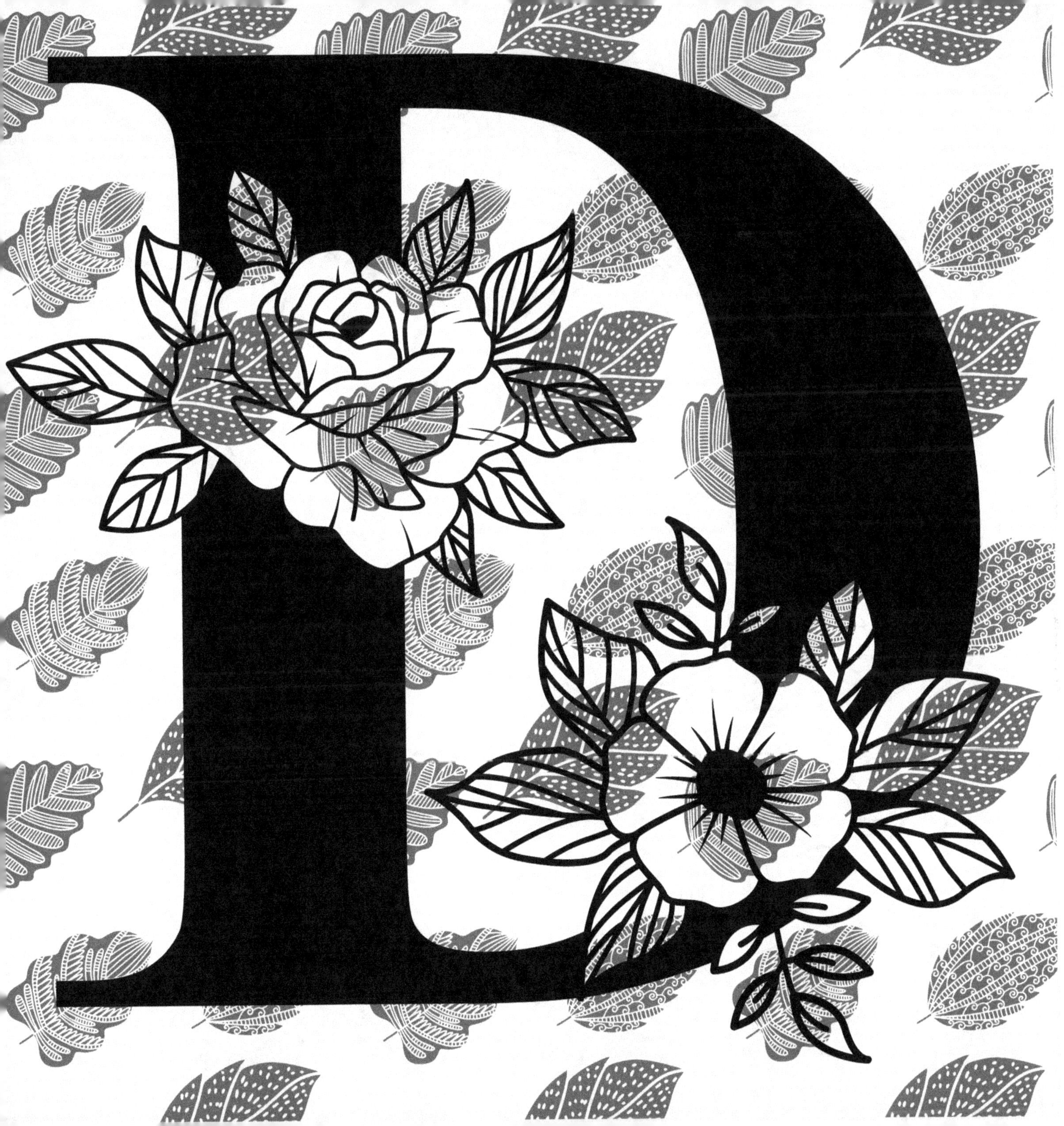

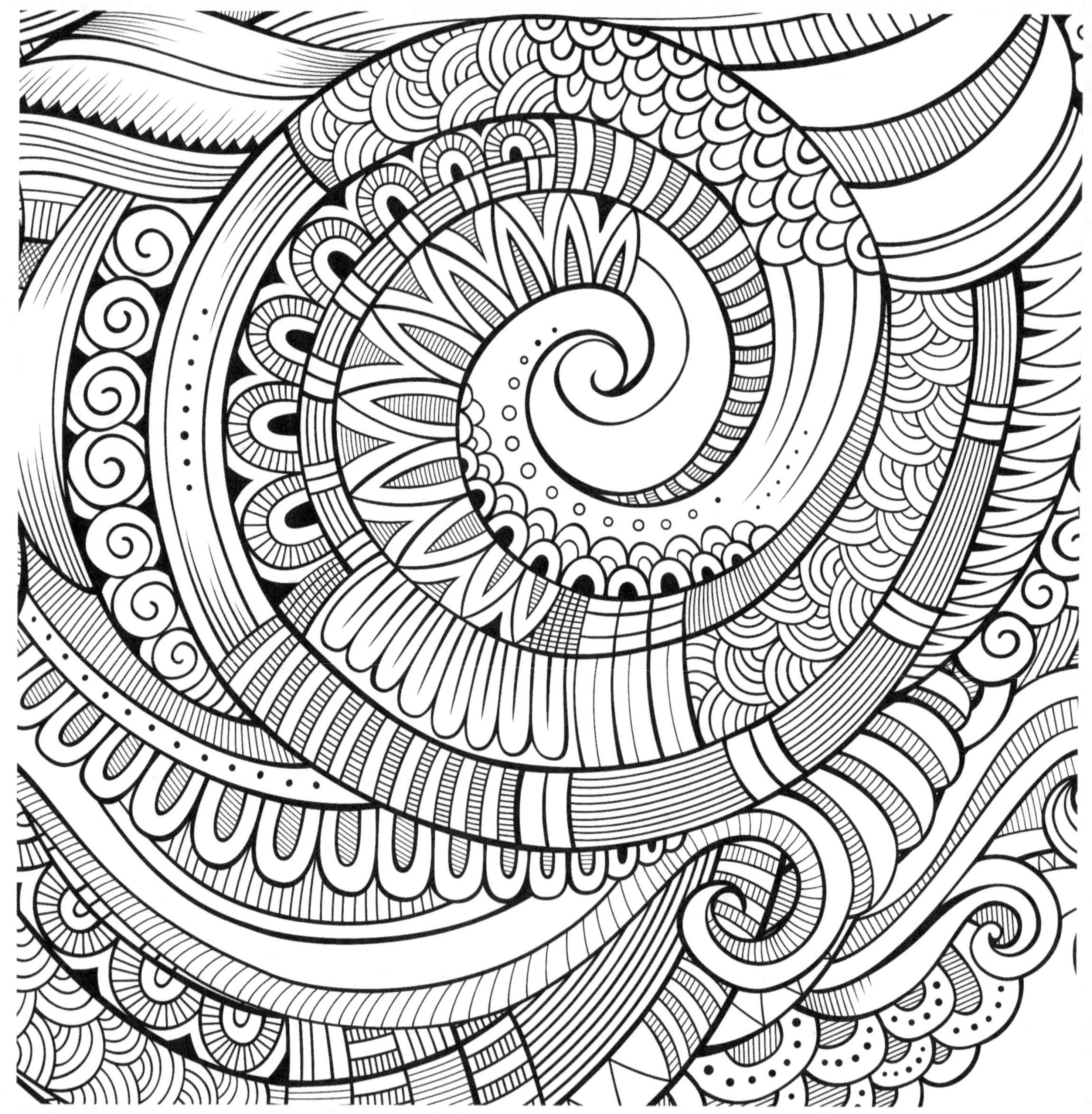

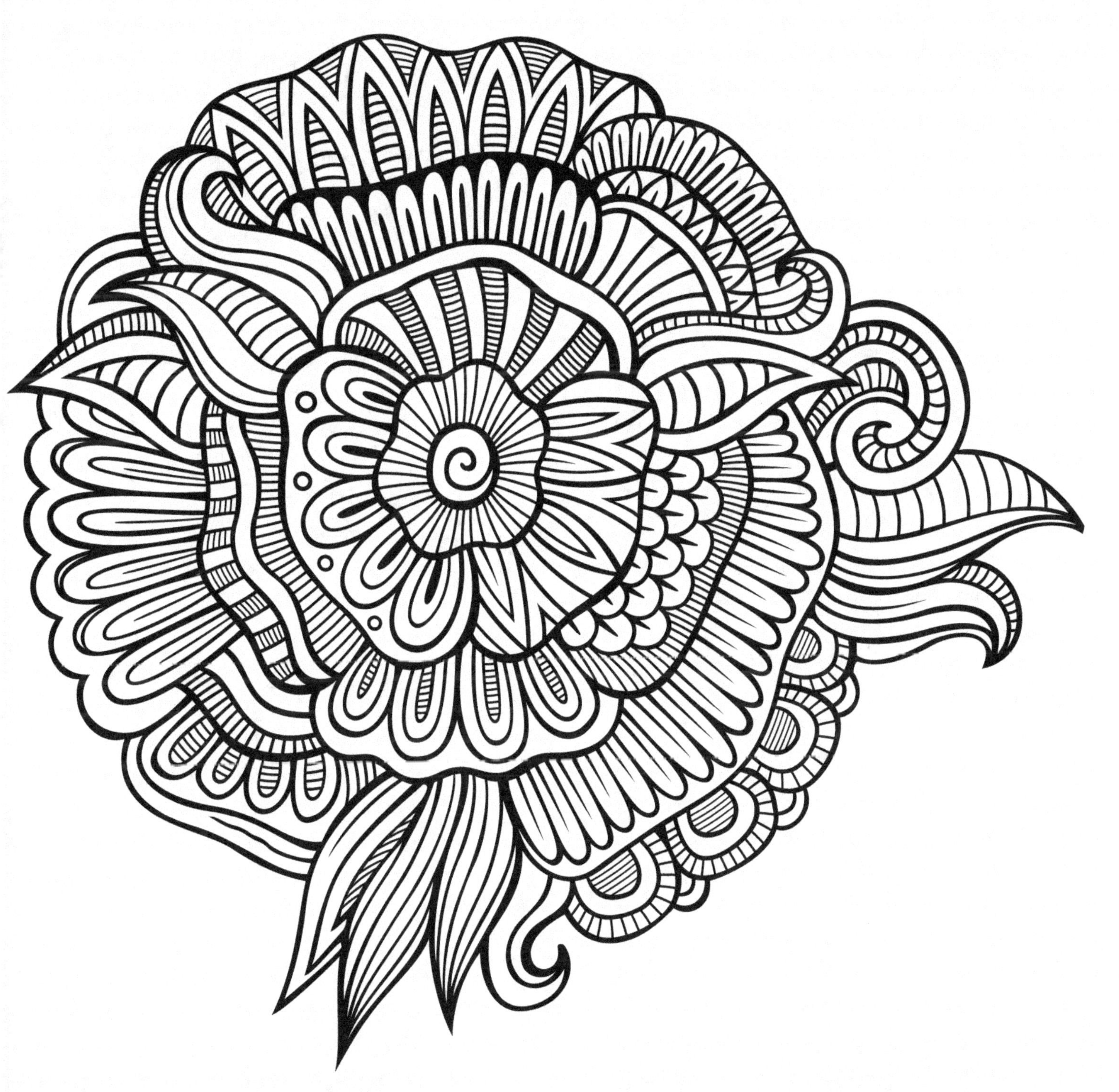

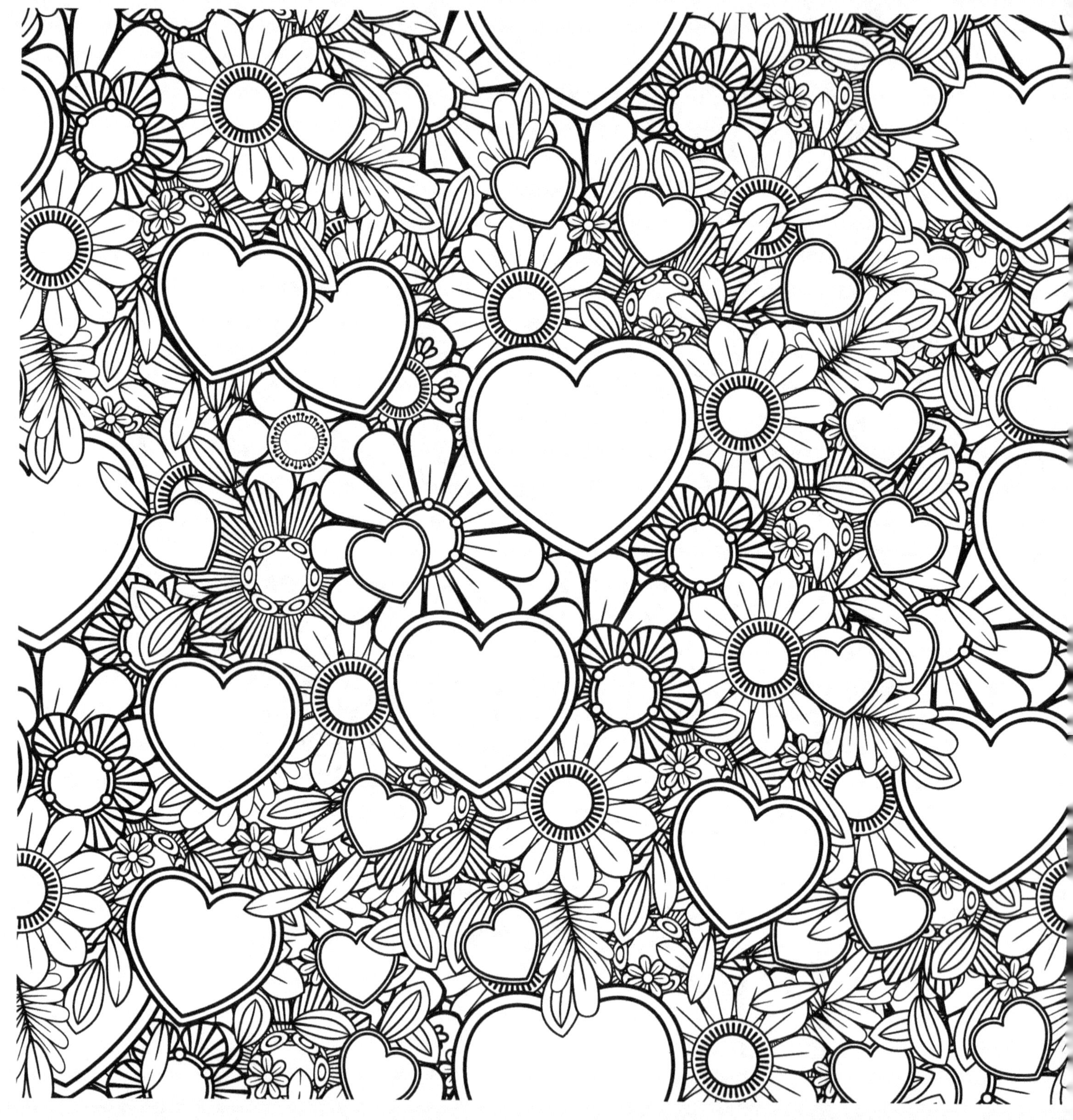

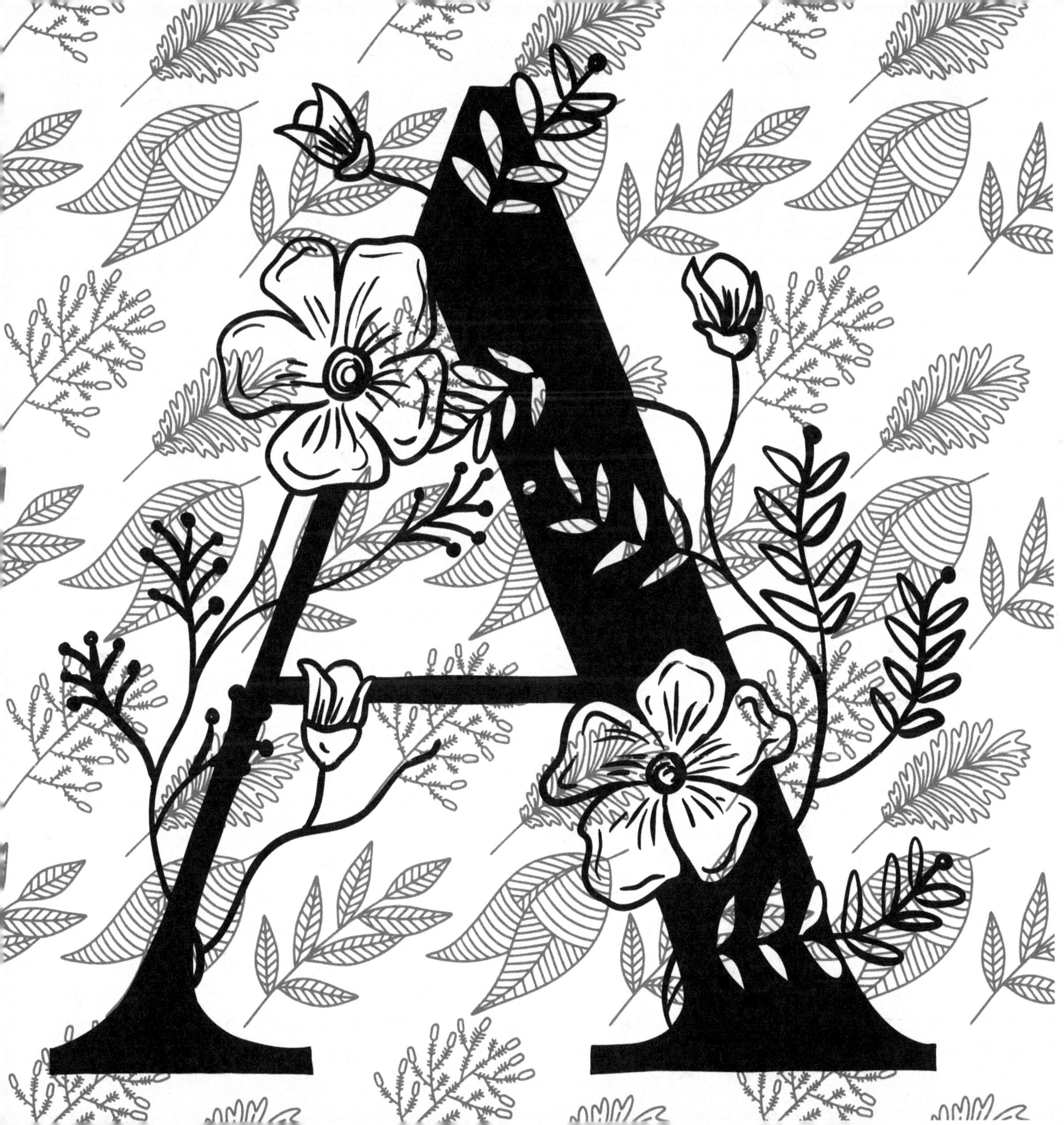

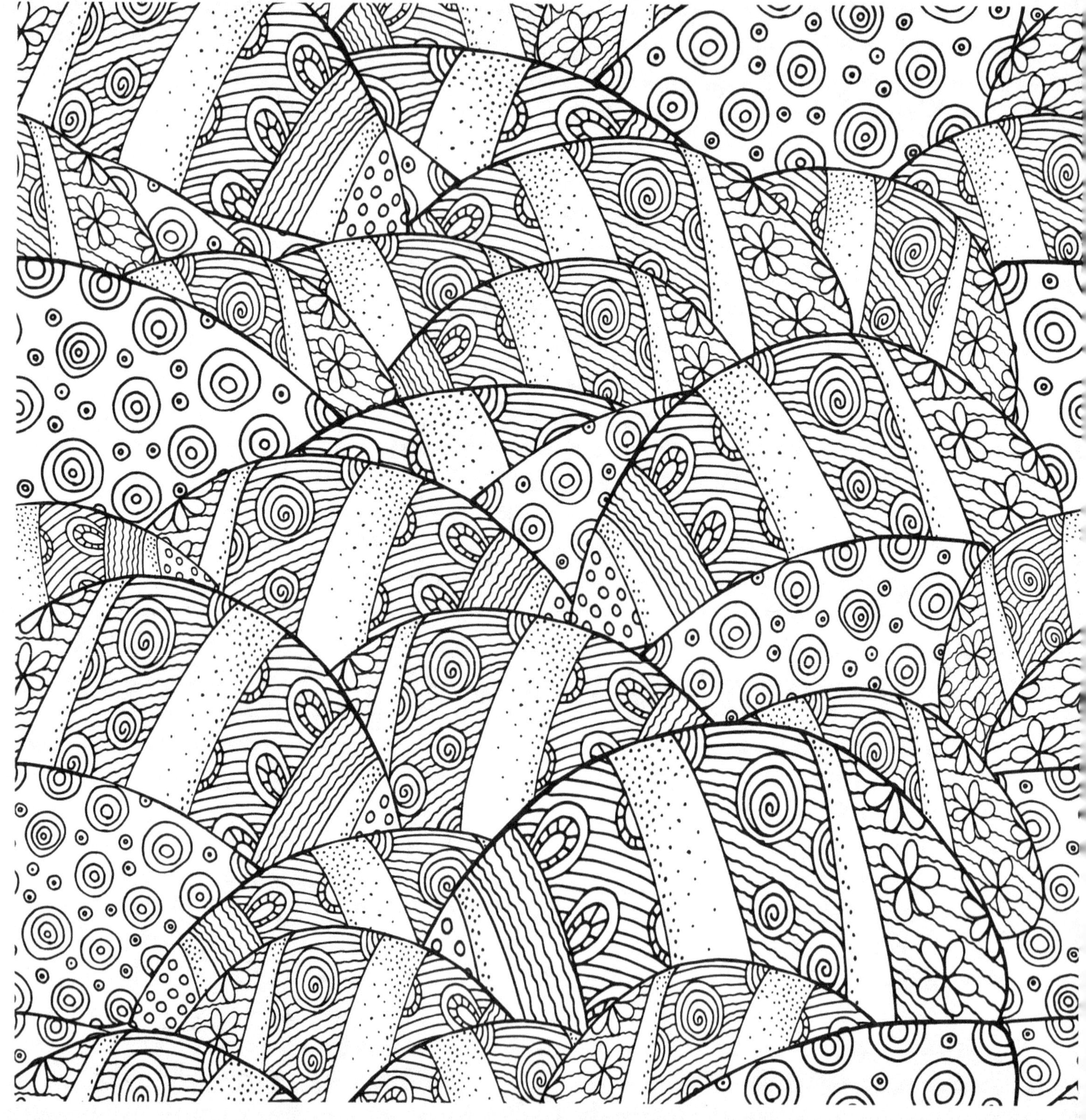

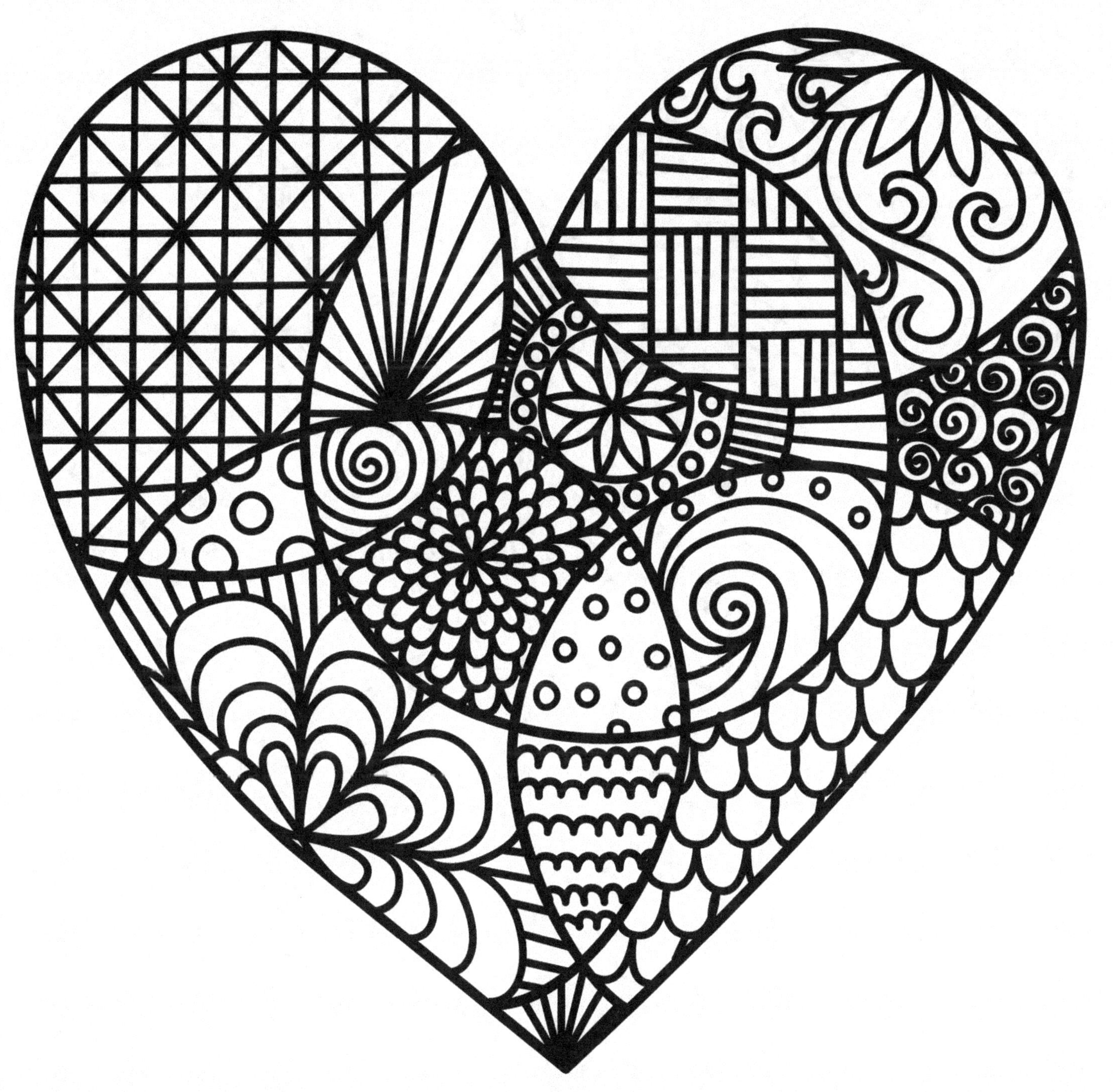

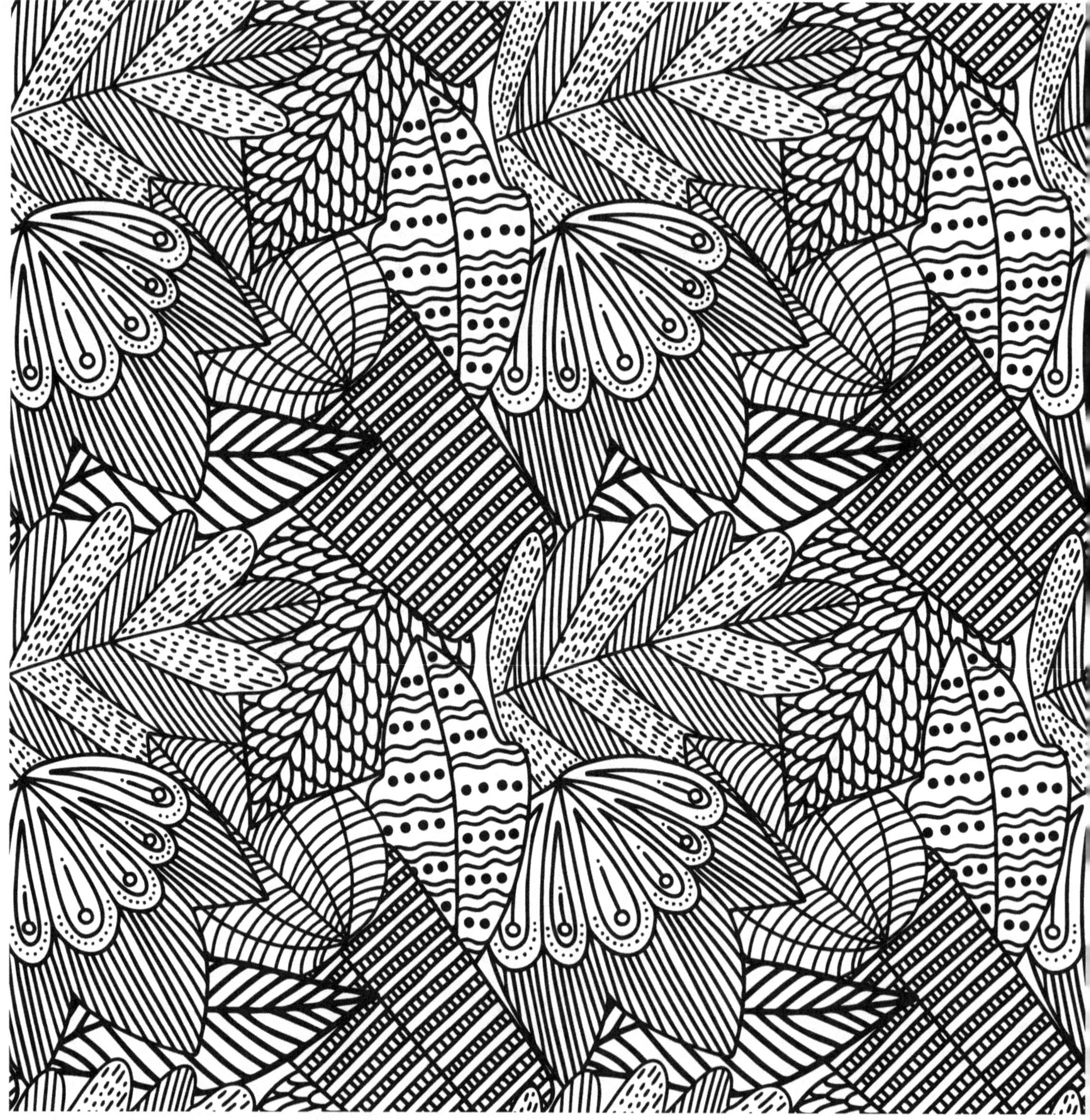

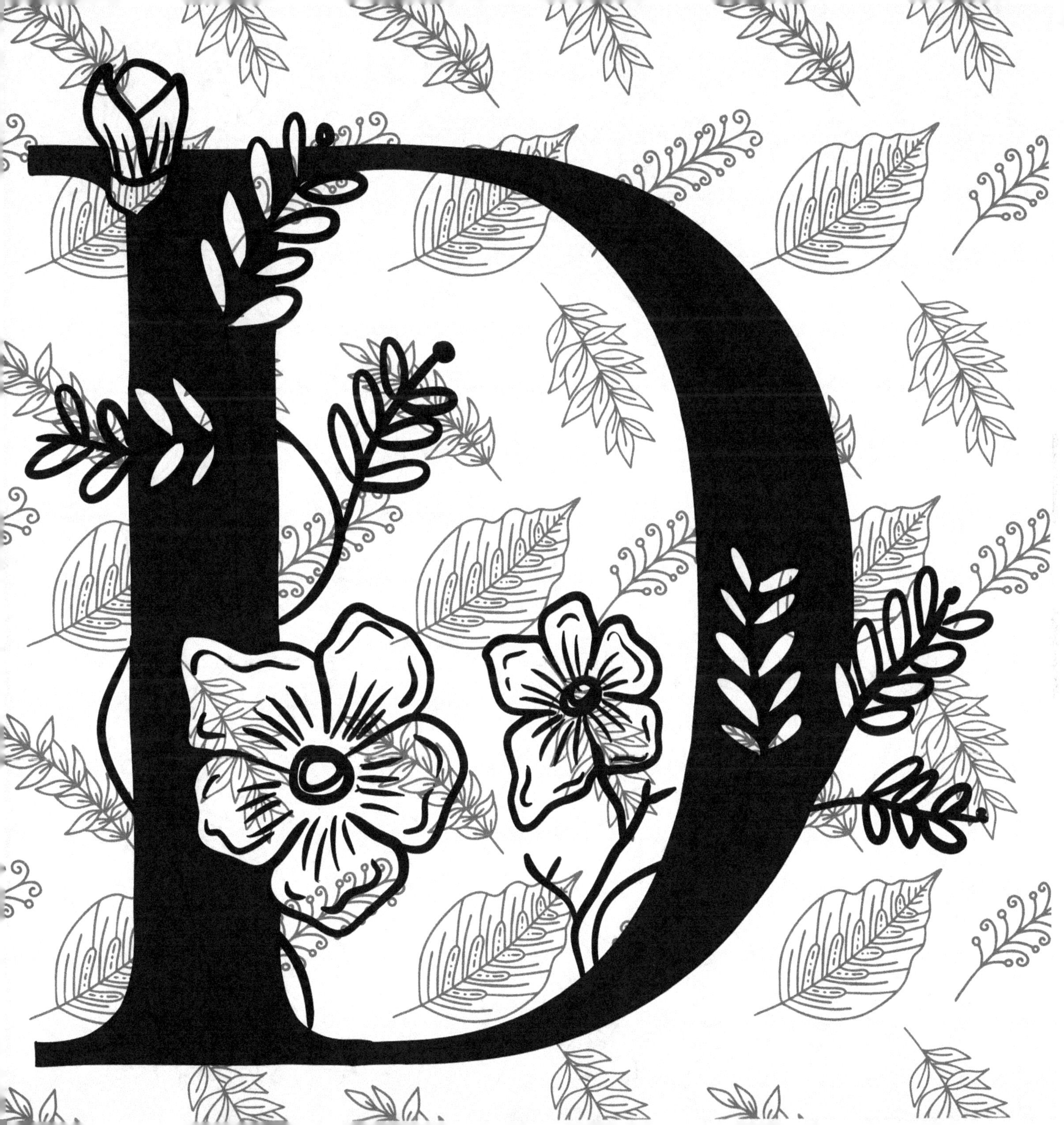

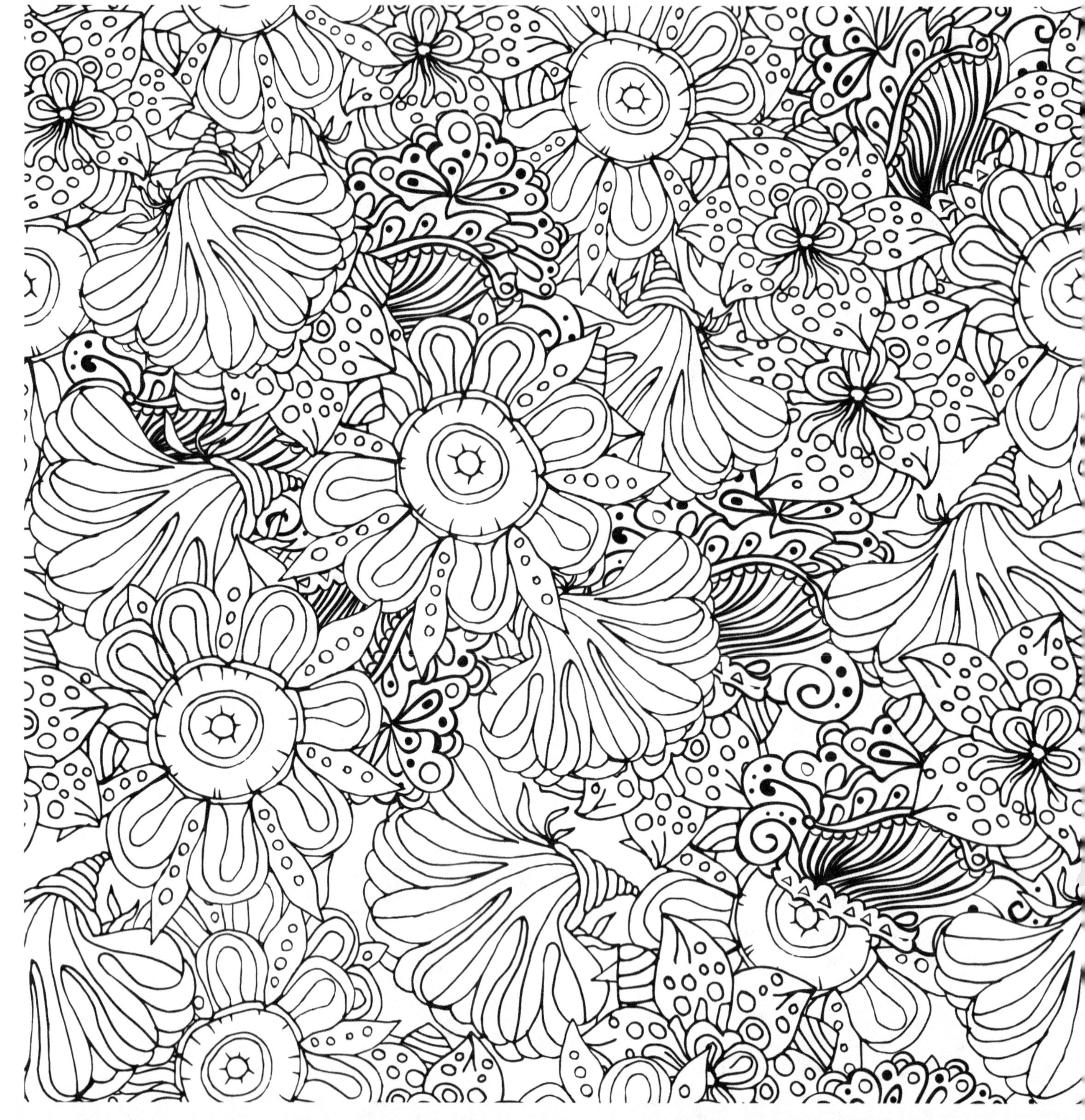

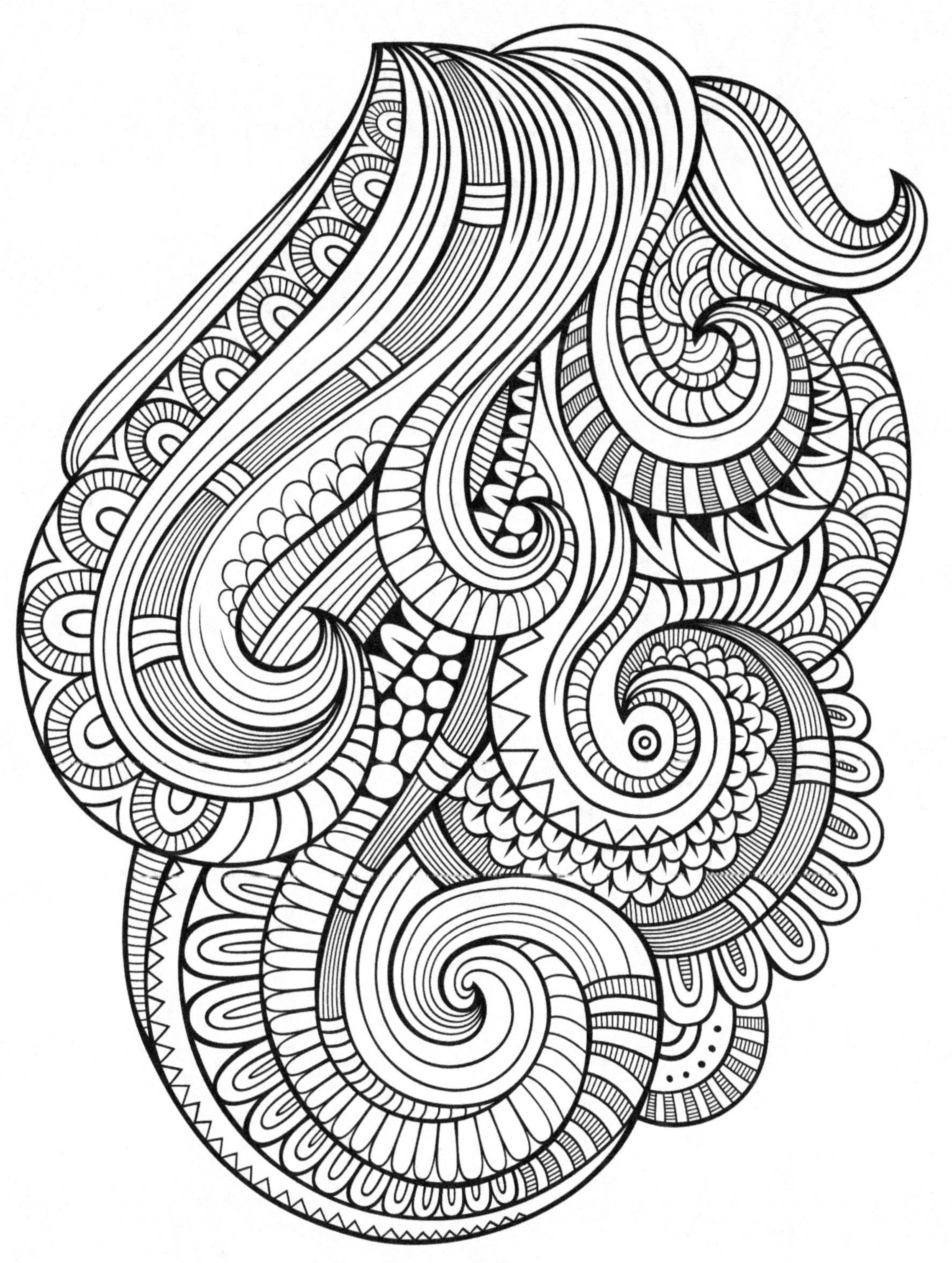

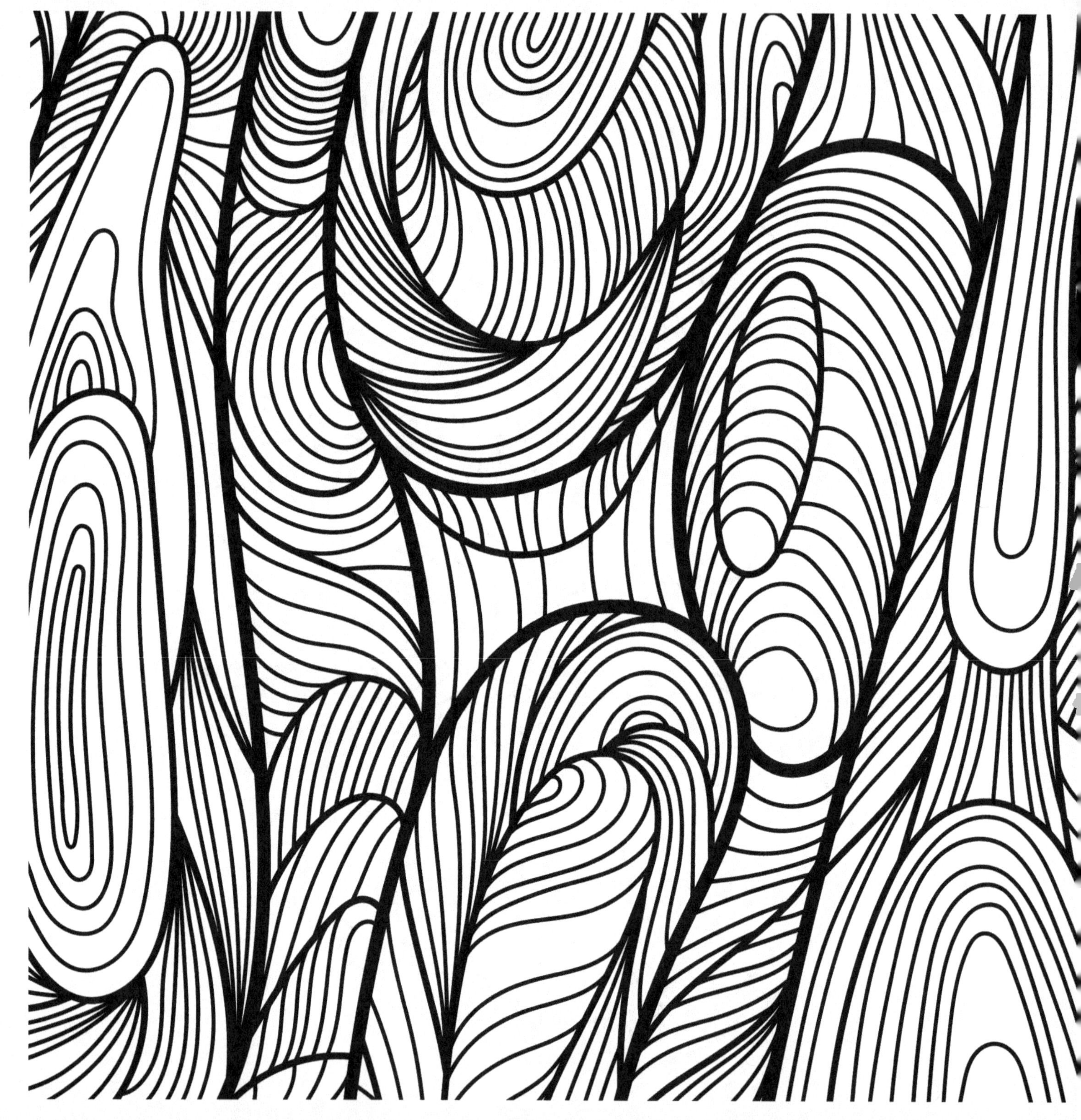

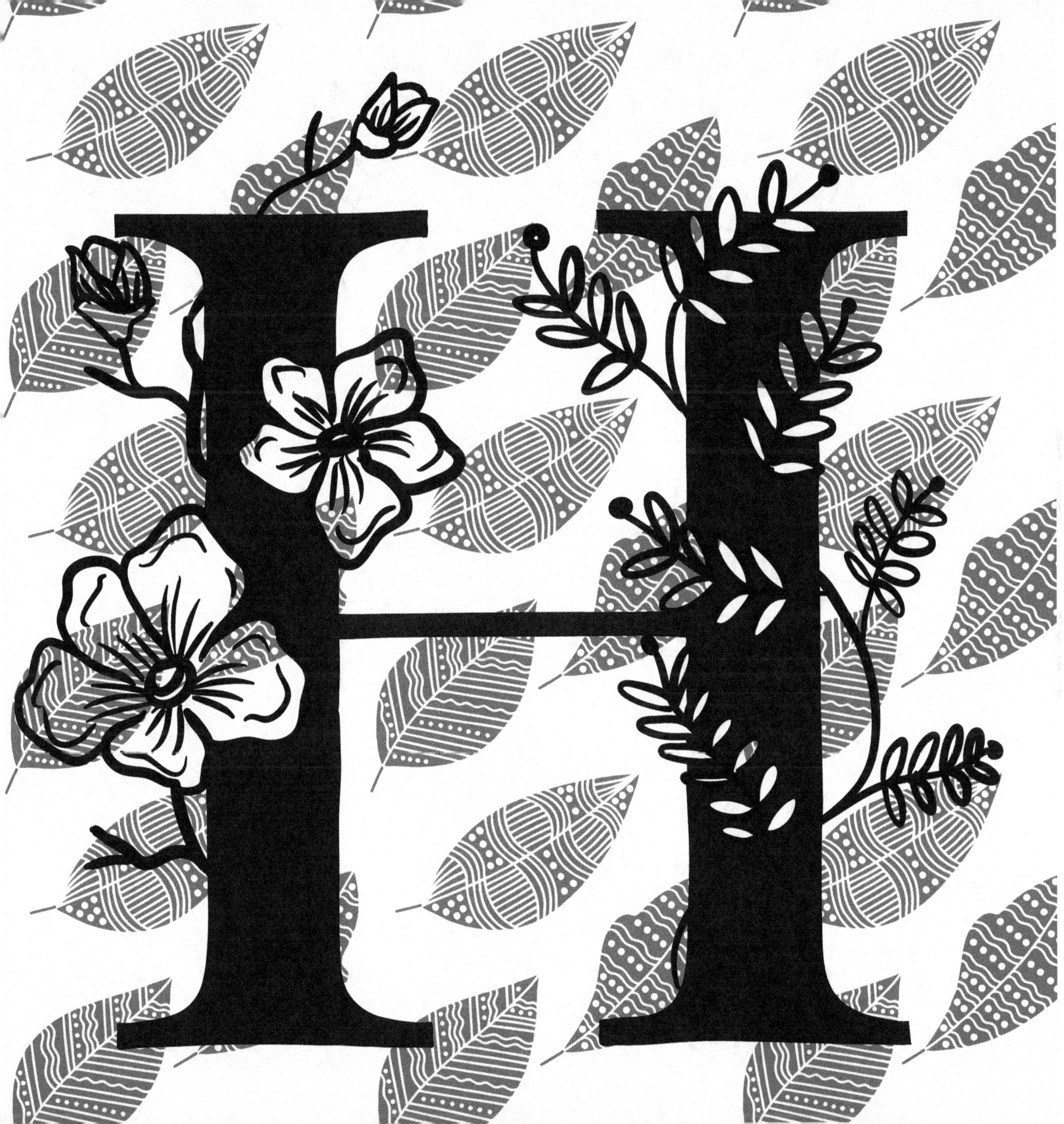

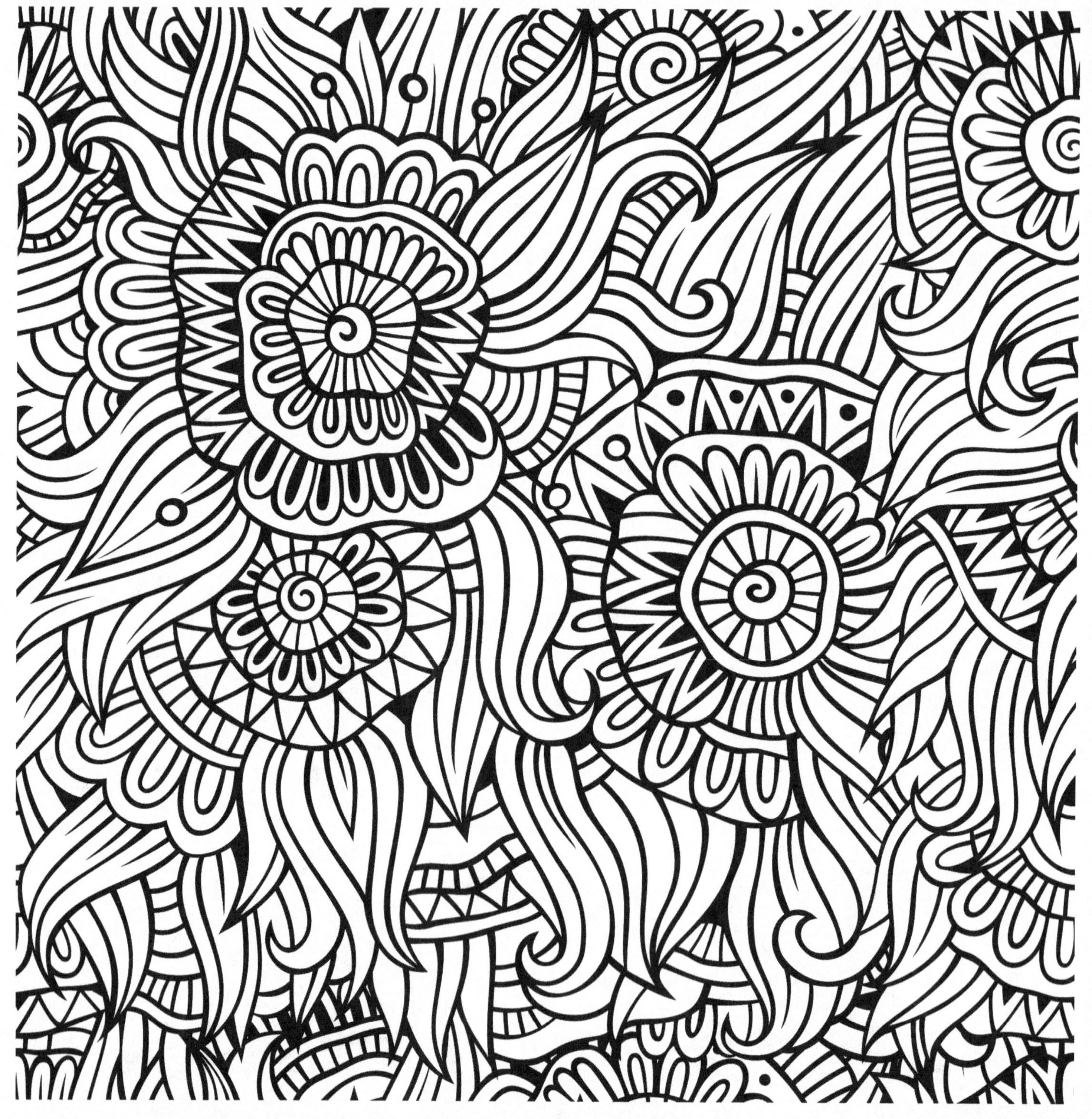

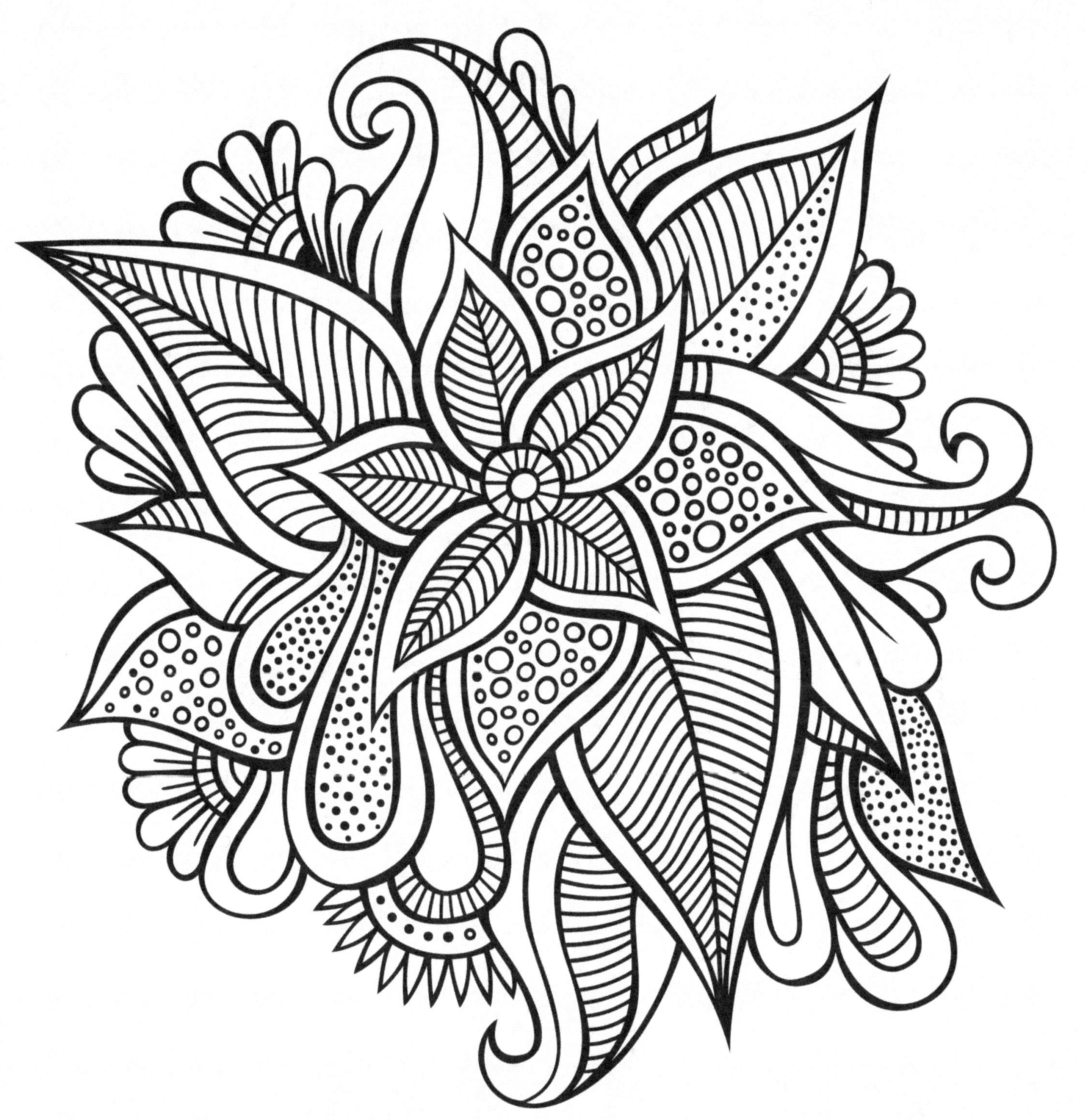

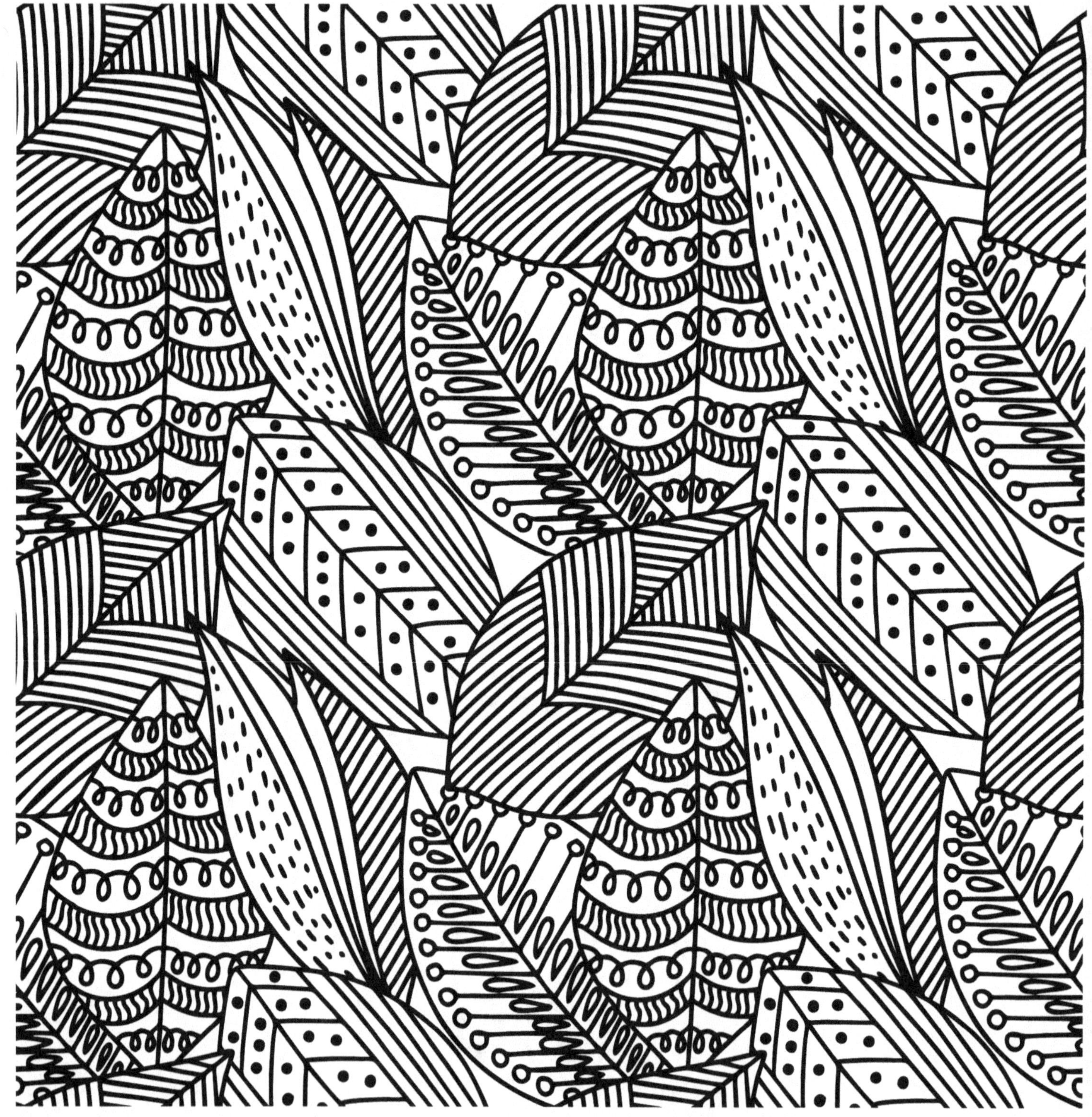

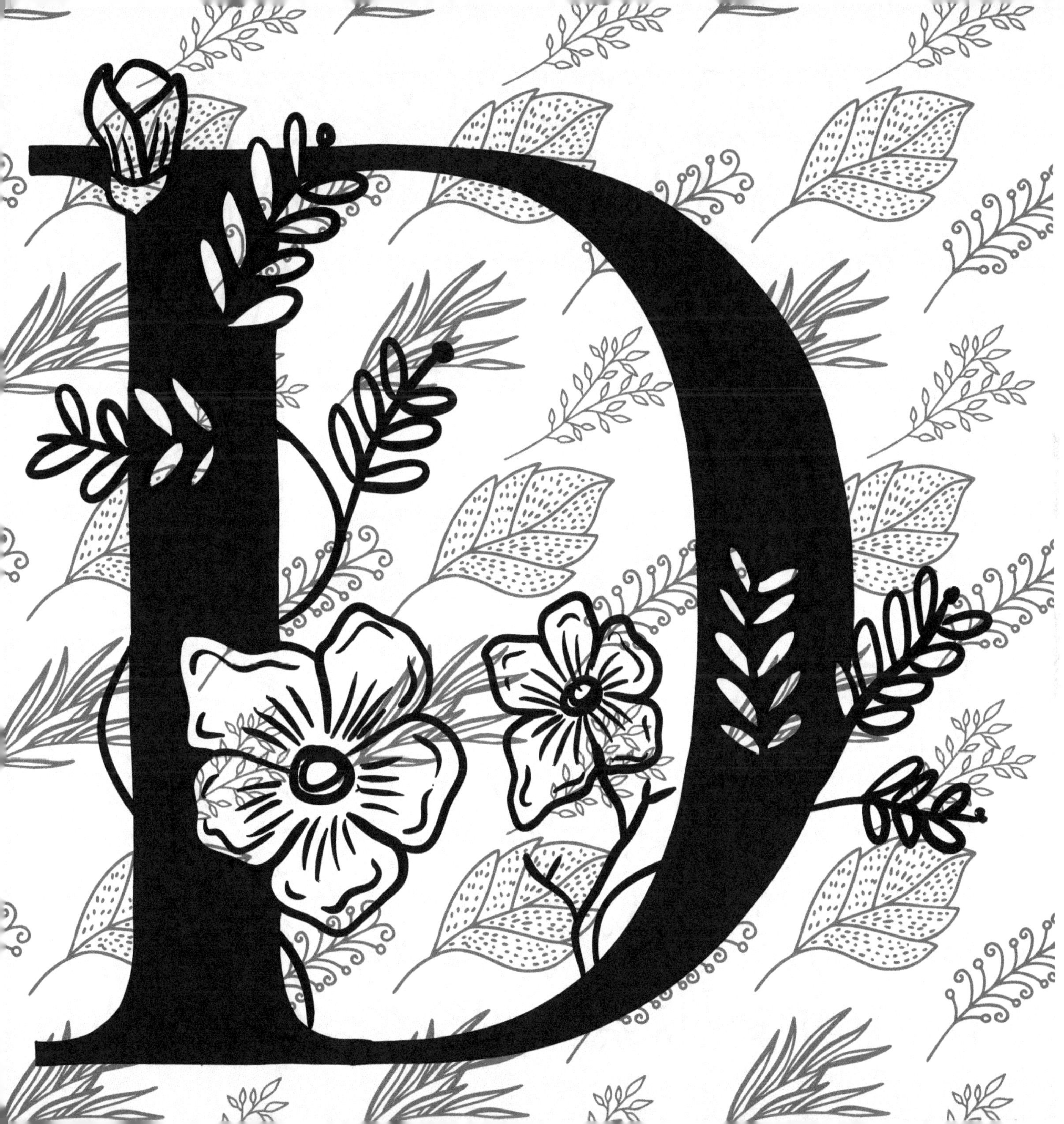

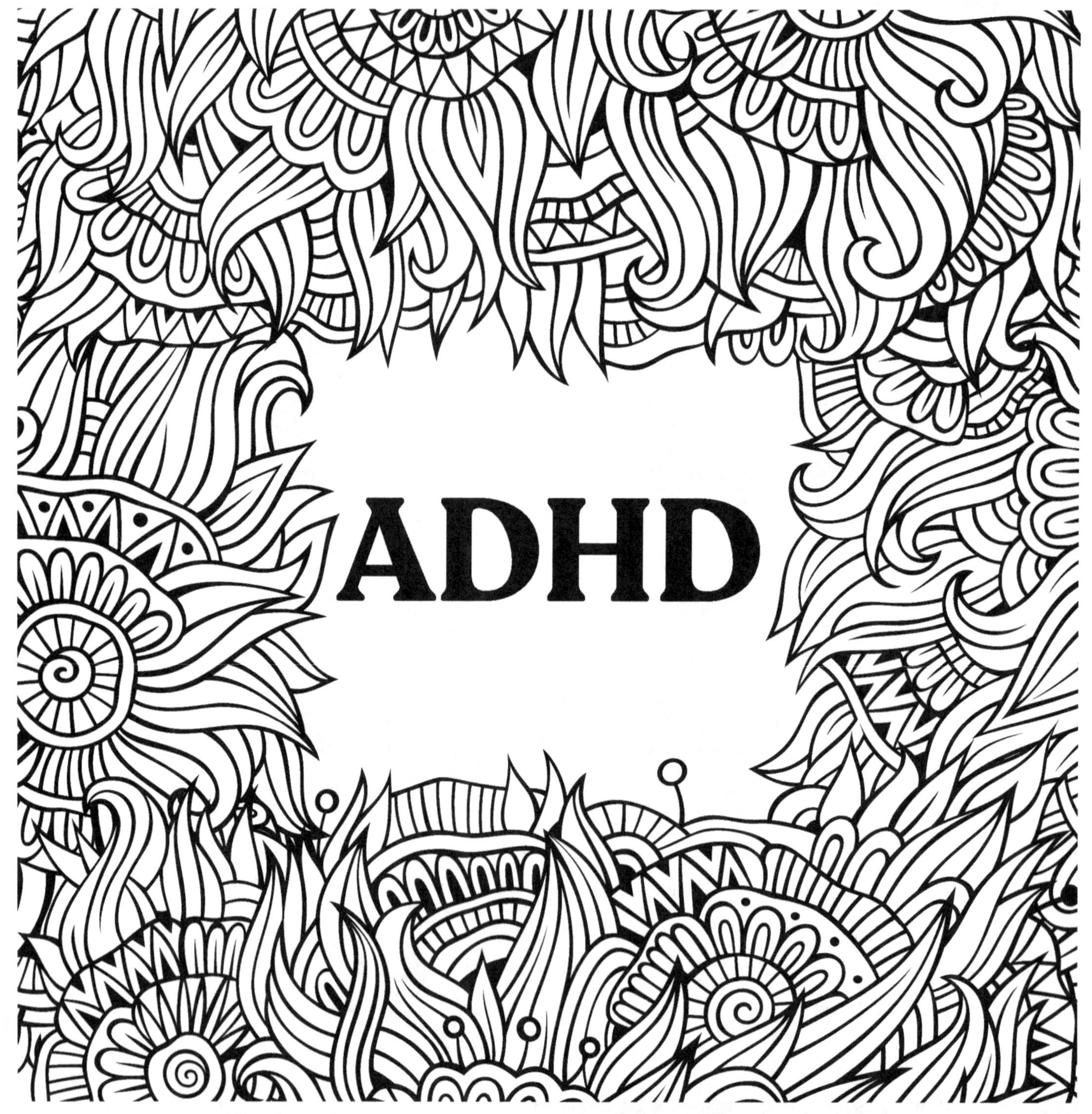
ADHD

www.ingramcontent.com/pod-product-compliance
Lightning Source LLC
LaVergne TN
LVHW081634120826
845149LV00025B/1910
* 9 7 9 8 9 9 2 1 9 2 9 3 3 *